teach yourself®

better chess

teach yourself®

better chess

william hartston

For over 60 years, more than 40 million people have learnt over 750 subjects the **teach yourself** way, with impressive results.

be where you want to be
with **teach yourself**

For UK order enquiries: please contact Bookpoint Ltd, 130 Milton Park, Abingdon, Oxon OX14 4SB. Telephone: +44 (0) 1235 827720. Fax: +44 (0) 1235 400454. Lines are open 09.00–18.00, Monday to Saturday, with a 24-hour message answering service. Details about our titles and how to order are available at www.teachyourself.co.uk

For USA order enquiries: please contact McGraw-Hill Customer Services, PO Box 545, Blacklick, OH 43004-0545, USA. Telephone: 1-800-722-4726. Fax: 1-614-755-5645.

For Canada order enquiries: please contact McGraw-Hill Ryerson Ltd, 300 Water St, Whitby, Ontario L1N 9B6, Canada. Telephone: 905 430 5000. Fax: 905 430 5020.

Long renowned as the authoritative source for self-guided learning – with more than 40 million copies sold worldwide – the **teach yourself** series includes over 300 titles in the fields of languages, crafts, hobbies, business, computing and education.

British Library Cataloguing in Publication Data: a catalogue record for this title is available from the British Library.

Library of Congress Catalog Card Number: on file.

First published in UK 1996 by Hodder Education, 338 Euston Road, London, NW1 3BH.

First published in US 1996 by Contemporary Books, a Division of the McGraw-Hill Companies, 1 Prudential Plaza, 130 East Randolph Street, Chicago, IL 60601 USA.

This edition published 2003.

Typeset by Transet Limited, Coventry, England.
Printed in Great Britain for Hodder Education, a division of Hodder Headline, 338 Euston Road, London NW1 3BH, by Cox & Wyman Ltd, Reading, Berkshire.

Hodder Headline's policy is to use papers that are natural, renewable and recyclable products and made from wood grown in sustainable forests. The logging and manufacturing processes are expected to conform to the environmental regulations of the country of origin.

Impression number 10 9 8 7 6 5 4
Year 2007 2006 2005

contents

**To the gentlemen of the RAC Chess Circle –
may your pawns never wither.**

introduction

Have you ever played through the moves of a chess game in a book or newspaper and come to a comment ending like this: '... and White, with his excellent control of the centre and rook established on the seventh rank, has a clear advantage'? Or perhaps: '... Black has excellent compensation for the sacrificed pawn.'

Do you accept such assessments at face value, or do you ask yourself just what is so good about controlling the centre, or having a rook on the seventh? And how do you measure the right amount of compensation to balance a pawn?

This book sets out to delve a little more deeply into the principles of good chess. For every easy-to-follow rule, there is an underlying meta-principle concerning the deeper laws of co-operation between pieces. Many of those meta-principles are generally lumped together under the illusory heading of 'positional judgement' or even 'intuition'. By explaining the ideas behind the elementary rules, and developing themes through the three sections of this book – Basic, Advanced and Mastery – I have tried to introduce the reader to the components that make up such judgement and intuition.

With concepts explained on left-hand pages and an example given on each facing page, the book is essentially a series of two-page lessons. While I have tried to arrange these roughly in order of increasing difficulty, each two-page spread is designed to be complete in itself. In other words, you may dip into it as you please, skipping sections or even jumping between the different levels of difficulty if you find it helpful to do so. All the same, there's a lot to be said for starting at the beginning and working through to the end.

Okay, that's enough introduction; let's get on with the game.

The material in this book falls into three sections: Basic, Advanced and Mastery, each comprising 25 lessons. Each section contains the building blocks of chess understanding needed to take one's play into higher reaches of comprehension and, with practice, effectiveness.

The base from which these lessons start, however, is not that of the beginner. This is not basic chess – which is covered in the companion volume *Teach Yourself Chess* – but basic better chess. You will recognize many of the concepts under discussion, but I hope you will here find them to be explored from a deeper perspective than before. Don't worry if the ideas seem unusual or even paradoxical. If good chess did not contain a wealth of logical paradoxes, then computers would have beaten all of us at it long ago. Even in the twenty-first century, human chess intuition can still give silicon precision a good run for its money. As I said before, let's get on with the game.

part one
basic

thinking

Most players believe that all calculation in chess is much the same. It's 'I go there, and he goes there, and I take that, and he recaptures ...' and so on. They don't realize it, but there are actually two distinct types of thinking going on: precise thinking and fuzzy thinking.

When it's your move in any position, there are likely to be some moves that just have to be calculated. Sequences of captures, or checks, or threats of mate, or attacks on undefended pieces have to be worked out in detail. Once they have been worked out, and you have identified the minefields and elephant traps lying in wait on the battlefield, then you can take time to enjoy the positional scenery and fumble your way through a few sequences of unforced moves to see what takes your fancy. The technique of thinking is simple:

> **First calculate the calculable.**

Captures and heavy threats force the opponent's reply. One must develop the technique to calculate such sequences through to the end, even if it is ten or twenty moves deep. Only when you've calculated the calculable, and no clearly advantageous continuation emerges, is it time to move into the fuzzy thought of looking for the most promising path through the forest of incalculable possibilities.

When you are still coming to terms with the complexities of the game, the best you can hope for is to recognize the forcing variations and work them through as well as you can. With experience, however, calculating the calculable becomes an almost automatic part of the technique of thinking. Then you can move on to the most fascinating aspect of the game: the interplay of strategy (fuzzy thought) and tactics (precise thought).

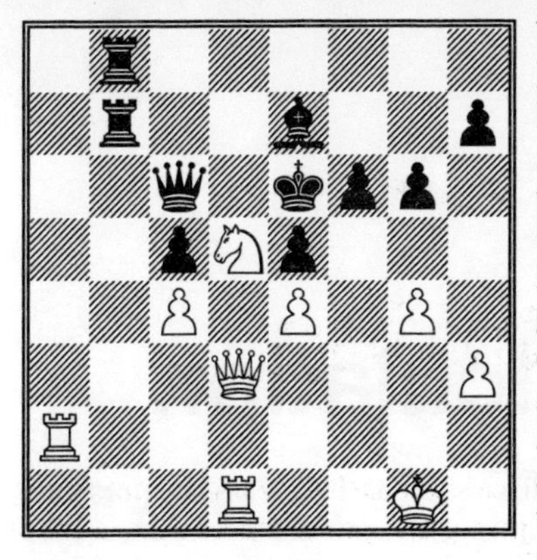

White to play and ... think! It's your move in this position. Explain your thoughts, both fuzzy and precise. In fuzzy terms, you're a pawn down, but with a beautifully placed knight on d5. You'd have good chances to draw the endgame if the queens and rooks were exchanged. Meanwhile, the black rooks are annoyingly active down the b-file and threatening to invade with 1...Rb3.

If you're feeling timid, you might consider 1.Ra3, then worry whether 1...Rb2 is a dangerous answer. If you're feeling aggressive, you might think about doubling your own rooks with 1.Rda1 to create the threat of 2.Ra6.

If you're properly in precise-thinking mode, however, you will find **1.Ra6!** (a forcing move which has to be looked at) **1...Qxa6 2.Nc7+!** (a check to continue the forcing variation) **2...Rxc7** (otherwise 3.Nxa6 leaves White queen for rook ahead) **3.Qd5 mate**. In practice, one should get the idea of such a combination through a bit of wishful thinking: 'If my knight were not on d5, and his queen were away from c6, then I could play Qd5 mate.' Combine that dream with the possibilities of Ra6 and Nc7+, and the answer should jump out.

Note that 1.Nc7+ is considerably less efficient. After 1...Qxc7 2.Qd5 Black is mated again, and after 1...Rxc7 2.Ra6! Black loses his queen for rook and knight, but after 1...Kf7! White has nothing to show for his adventure.

calculation

It's very easy to miss a good move such as 1.Ra6 on the previous page. If you find yourself thinking, 'I can't do that because he takes my rook', then you've fallen into a thought process that is fundamentally lazy. What you should be thinking is: 'I can't move my rook to a6, because after he takes it with his queen, I have no good reply.'

The thoughts sound very similar, but there is a big difference: in the first, faulty version, you stop thinking when the black queen is still on c6. As soon as she glares at your rook, it is frightened off. In the second version, you force yourself not only to think about the position when the queen has arrived at a6, but you even cast your mind's eye around the board for a good move for White after that. The lesson is simple, and an important part of mental discipline:

> Always look one move deeper than seems to be necessary.

After any sequence of captures or checks, look for the sting in the tail. Just when the forcing moves appear to have come to an end, there may be a little piece of subtle violence that puts a completely different complexion on the position. The tactics do not always end when the captures and checks run out.

On a related point, you must also train yourself (and this is far more difficult) to look for winning combinations for your opponent too. Playing on the white side of the previous diagram, you may congratulate yourself if you found 1.Ra6, but now turn the board round and think of it from Black's point of view. Suppose, on the previous move, Black had moved his rook from c8 to b8. A very plausible move – the rook was doing nothing active on c8, and now it is helping its colleague create threats on the b-file. Yet it loses, as we have seen, to the combination with Ra6 and Nc7+. Would you have spotted it?

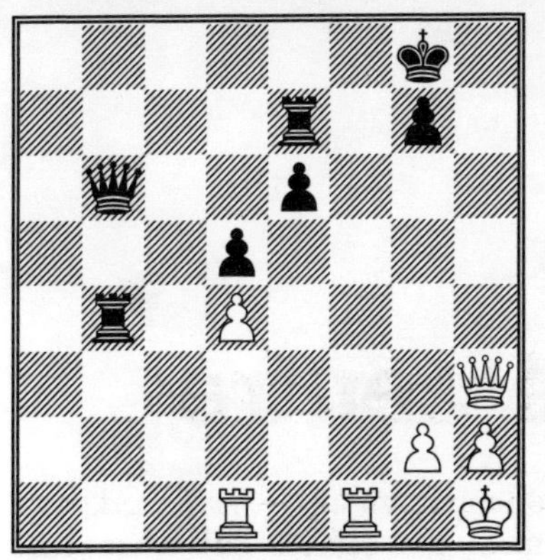

It's White to play in this position and, with material level and his d-pawn attacked, his hopes of winning must lie in an attack on the black king. One idea might be 1.Ra1 or 1.Rc1, threatening a fatal check on the back rank; another idea could be 1.Rf4, intending to bring the rook to h4 to chase the black king into the open with Rh8+.

But first there's something else that needs to be analysed. White can force the play with **1.Rf8+** (without a cry of, 'I can't do that because he'll take my rook') **Kxf8 2.Qh8+ Kf7 3.Rf1+ Kg6.**

Is that it? It is not difficult to dispose of 4.Qe8+ Rxe8 or 4.Rf6+ gxf6 (Kxf6 is also good) 5.Qg8+ Kf5 and the king runs away, so is it time to go back to some fuzzy thinking beginning with 1.Rc1 or 1.Ra1, or have we overlooked something?

Think again about the position after 3...Kg6. Black's king is so exposed that it ought to take only a small nudge to push it to its doom. The important thing is that Black has no important threats – not even a single check – which gives White a spare move.

The winning move is **4.g4!** after which Black is helpless against the threat of **5.Qh5 mate**. In the position after 3...Kg6, all the signposts are there: an exposed king, a queen and rook in fine attacking positions, and a small army of black pieces cut off from the defence of their own king, yet it is surprisingly easy to stop analysing after 3...Kg6, simply because there is no forcing check or capture.

Such things are so much easier to see when they appear in diagrams with the words 'White to play and win' beneath them. The art of good tactics is to develop your own antennae which start twitching automatically when such a position arrives on the board during a game.

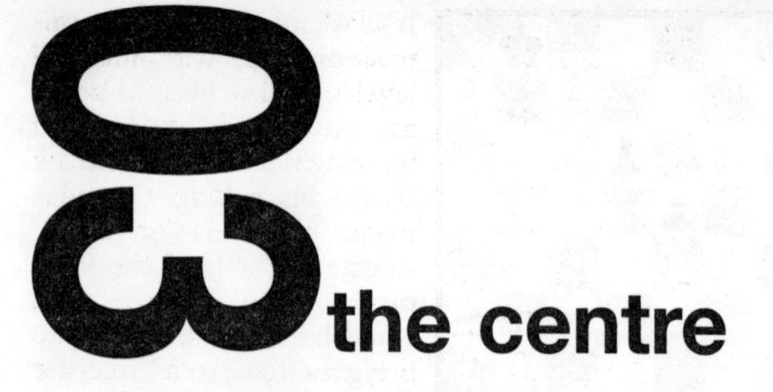

03 the centre

The primary objective of the opening, you may have read, is to develop your pieces and control the centre. But what does 'control of the centre' really mean, and why is it so important?

When the game begins, the two sides are in compact formations on their back two ranks. The opening phase is a fight for terrain over the four ranks separating the two armies. When your opponent advances in one direction, you may either try to drive him back (or at least prevent his further advance), or seize territory elsewhere. Some games develop with White advancing on the K-side and Black on the Q-side; or one player may dominate the black squares and the other the white squares. While the battle-lines are being drawn up, however, the centre is the sensible place to be. A piece – especially a knight – can influence play on both wings from a central outpost, and the side that has use of the central squares may most easily switch his forces from one wing to another. The important thing is to maintain lines of communication, and the side that has the use of the central squares is more likely to be able to do so.

Later, when the time is right to attack the enemy king, or to push a pawn majority, the centre may become less important, but in the early stages of the game, the centre is the most important part of the board.

> Control of the centre is the key to flexibility.

There are two basic ways to gain control of the centre:

- occupy the centre with pawns, and advance them systematically to enable pieces to occupy the squares behind them;
- tempt your opponent's pawns forward in the centre, then snipe at them from a distance to force them to advance, leaving weaknesses behind them.

Some of the best strategic battles occur when the two strategies meet.

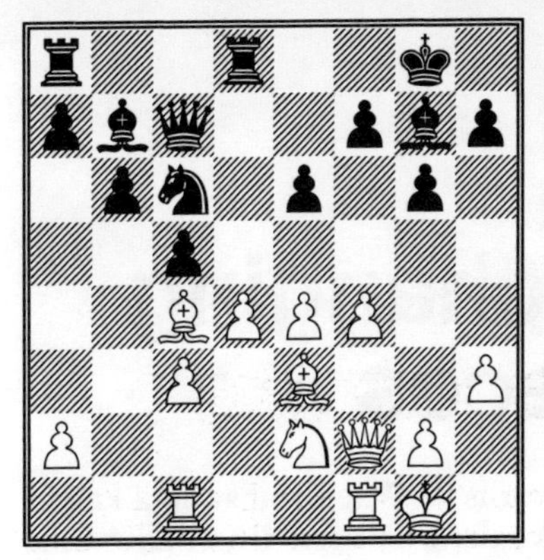

A clash of central strategies from the game Gligoric–Smyslov, Kiev 1959. White has occupied the centre with his pawns at d4, e4 and f4; Black has tried to control it from a distance. With his last move, 15.Qf2, White has provided his d-pawn with added support while preparing to open lines for attack with f5. Has White's central strategy triumphed?

Look at what happened next: **15...Na5** (unveiling a threat to the e-pawn as well as attacking the bishop) **16.Bd3 f5!** (putting more pressure on the centre while also stopping the white f-pawn from advancing) **17.e5 c4 18.Bc2 Nc6** (having done its job on a5, the knight returns to the central arena) **19.g4 Ne7! 20.Kh2 Qc6 21.Ng3 b5**.

The battle is only just beginning, but Black has come off far better in the battle for the centre. His knight is ready to occupy d5 and influence the play on both wings, while his queen and bishop on the long diagonal point menacingly from one corner of the board to the other. White's pawns have advanced to occupy the centre, but he has lost control of the squares behind them. Note how Black maintained perfect communication between the two sides of the board despite his modest initial stance in the centre.

04 exchanging pieces

Fair exchange is no robbery – or is it? When you swap a knight for a knight, or exchange rooks along an open file, or allow one bishop on each side to disappear from the board, the transaction may seem perfectly balanced, but even the most equitable-seeming exchange may greatly favour one side or the other.

Consider, before consenting to any exchange, which of the men about to be sent back to the box is doing a more effective job. It is likely to be advantageous to exchange pieces when:

- you have more pawns than your opponent, but the pieces* are otherwise level – an extra pawn increases in value the fewer pieces are on the board;
- you have a cramped position and the swapping off of one piece can create much-needed manoeuvring space.

The most important thing, however, before consenting to an exchange is to think about the pieces that will remain on the board. Are you about to lose a crucial member of your army?

> Weak players assess a position by counting the captured men; strong players consider only the men remaining on the board.

You can save yourself a great deal of effort, and avoid making potentially costly mistakes, by simply looking at the respective roles of each piece before agreeing to an exchange. Often, you ought not to be calculating variations at all. When an exchange of pieces is offered, the decision may often be made purely on static considerations. The question to ask is: 'Will he miss his piece more than I'll miss mine?' It is frequently said that exchanges ease the defender, yet many games have been lost through permitting the exchange of a vital defensive piece, or by allowing an attacker to simplify into a winning endgame.

*Throughout this book, the term 'piece' is used to mean queen, rook, knight or bishop. Where pawns are included, the term is 'man'.

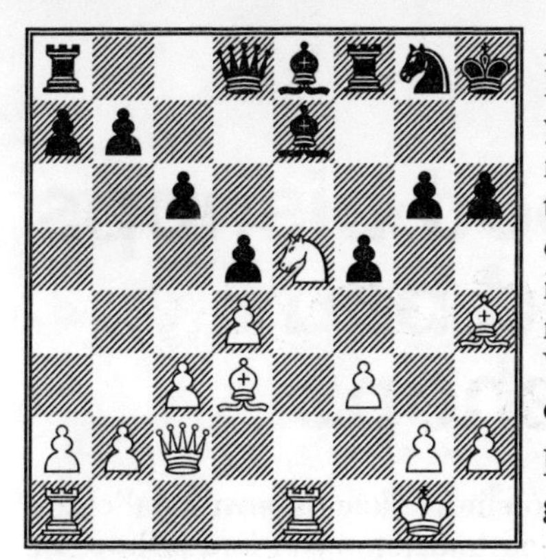

A position spotted in an English county match some years ago. Black has just retreated his knight from f6 to g8, offering an exchange of bishops. White now sank into deep thought, then retreated his bishop to f2. Was he right to avoid the exchange?

His reasoning must have gone like this.

- If my opponent offered the exchange, then he must want to get rid of the bishops. If that's what he wants, why should I let him?
- Anyway, my bishop's going to be useful attacking his weak black squares.
- If I take on e7, his knight will recapture, and emerge from its passive square on g8.

Faulty on all counts! The first point falls into the trap of assuming that your opponent knows what he is doing – which is rarely the case; the second point missed the fact that Black's own bishop is far more essential to the defence of the black squares than White's is in attacking them; the third point confuses short-term considerations with long-term objectives.

With his pawns on c6, d5, f5 and g6, Black has undeniably been neglecting his black squares. White has control of a splendid central square at e5, and Black has no comparable outpost. Black's bishop on e7 is his principal black-square draught excluder. When it is exchanged, the battle for the black squares is over.

In fact, after 1.Bxe7 Nxe7 2.h4! the threat of a disruptive h5 is always lurking over Black's position and White has a large advantage, but that is not relevant to the decision to exchange bishops. Just think 'His bishop is more useful to him than mine is to me' and whip it off.

5 good bishops and bad bishops

The bad bishop is the most common cliché of positional chess. It is also the most frequently misunderstood. A bad bishop, we are told, is one that is impeded by its own pawns. If your bishop is travelling on the white squares and most of your pawns are also on white squares, it stands to reason that the pawns are likely to get in the way of the bishop, especially if the bishop finds itself locked in behind the pawns.

The real problem of the bad bishop, however, is not the bishop itself, which may be perfectly effective defending some weak pawns, or as an attacking piece, emphasizing the white-square control that the pawns bring. No, the real problem lies on the other half of the board. When your pawns and your bishop are both on white squares, what is going to look after the black ones?

> Don't blame the bad bishop; blame its colleague who isn't there to guard your weak squares.

Bad bishops are liable to lose endgames against good bishops or knights, not because they are abnormally restricted, but because of the absence of any defence to an invasion by the enemy king, or some other piece, on the squares the bishop was not designed to control. Your pawns on white squares, for example, can restrict your opponent's white-squared bishop as much as they hamper your own. It's the black squares you have to worry about.

The great 18th-century French player Philidor advised putting your pawns on the same colour as your bishop on the flank where you are defending, but on the opposite colour on the side where you plan to attack. A bad bishop can be a good defender.

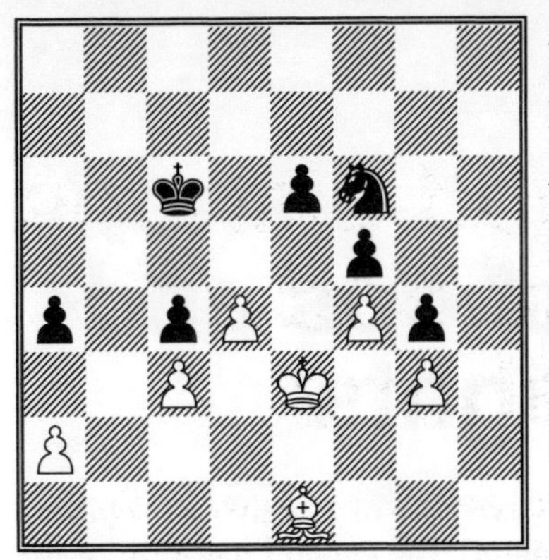

A classic case of a bad bishop, from the game Henneberger-Nimzowitsch, 1931. It is Black to play. White's bishop is completely passive, but it is not clear how Black can make progress. He would like to chase the white king away from e3, then advance with his own king to e4, eventually squeezing in to f3 or d3 to join the knight in a decisive attack on the g- or c-pawn. The trouble is that the only ways to chase the king from e3 involve putting the black knight at d5 or e4, right in the patch that Black's king wants to follow.

Now watch and see how Nimzowitsch accomplished the task:

1...Ne4! 2.Ke2 (the bishop cannot move without losing either the g-pawn or c-pawn) **2...Kd5 3.Ke3 Kd6! 4.Ke2 Kc6 5.Ke3 Kd5 6.Ke2 Nd6!** (the knight frees e4 and comes round to attack the c-pawn from a different direction) **7.Ke3 Nb5 8.Bd2 Na3! 9.Bc1** (There was no choice: 9.Be1 Nc2+ 10.Kd2 Nxe1 11.Kxe1 Ke4 12.Ke2 a3! forces the white king to step aside and allow Black to invade at d3 or f3.) **9...Nb1! 10.Bb2 a3! 11.Ba1** (11.Bc1 Nxc3 12.Bxa3 Nxa2 wins for Black without great difficulty).

Black has cornered the white bishop, but run his own knight out of moves. This is the position he has been aiming for all along, but how does he now make progress? The answer is delightful:

11...Kd6! 12.Ke2 (12.Kf2 loses to 12...Nd2 13.Kg2 Nb3! 14.axb3 axb3) **12...Kc6! 13.Kd1** (the best chance, since 13.Ke3 Kd5 14.Ke2 Ke4 is hopeless) **13...Kd5 14.Kc2 Ke4 15.Kxb1 Kf3.**

Black has achieved his objective and is now ready to capture on g3 and push his g-pawn home, but the game is not over yet:

16.Bb2! axb2! (after 16...Kxg3 17.Bxa3, the bad bishop joins in the game after Bc5 and d5) **17.a4 Kxg3 18.a5 Kh2! 19.a6 g3 20.a7 g2 21.a8=Q g1=Q+ 22.Kxb2 Qg2+!** (this explains why Black did not play 18...Kxf4) **23.Qxg2+ Kxg2 24.Ka3 Kf3 25.Kb4 Kxf4 26.Kxc4 Ke3 27.d5 exd5+ 28.Kxd5 f4** and **White resigned**. He loses the pawn race by a single move.

09 bishops and knights

We have just seen an extreme example of a truly awful bishop struggling against a nimble knight. The general question of the relative strengths of bishop and knight is a complex one. Some say that bishops are better than knights in open positions, and knights are superior in closed ones. Others maintain that it's all a question of how many pawns remain on the board. But open positions may become blocked; closed positions may burst into life, and many pawns may become few after some exchanges.

The truth is simpler and more obvious. Just look at the way they move: knights can get anywhere, given the time; bishops can move at great speed – one move where the knight takes six to cross the board from corner to corner – but the bishop can only ever reach half the squares on the board. The key point is that a bishop may simultaneously influence play on both sides of the board. If there are two emergencies to attend to, the knight can only offer a slow shuttle service.

> If there is active play happening on both wings, and no pawns are blocking the centre, then a bishop is stronger than a knight.

All this has two practical implications.

- If the central pawns are blocked and look like remaining so, you should be happy to exchange your bishops for knights.
- If you are playing with a bishop against a knight, try to exchange central pawns, and create something to think about on both wings.

The bishop is most noticeably superior to a knight in an endgame where the players have passed pawns on opposite sides of the board. The bishop can then help shepherd its own pawn forwards, while also looking in the other direction to prevent the opponent's pawn from rushing ahead. The knight has to choose whether to attack or defend.

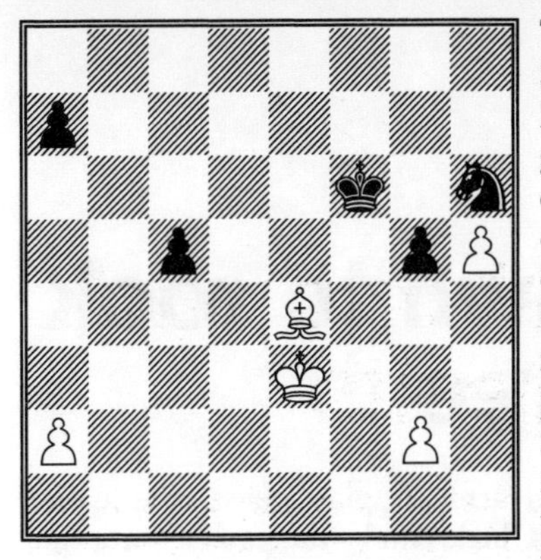

This endgame, from Spassky–Fischer, Santa Monica 1966, provides as good an example as one could want of the superiority of bishop over knight in an open position with play on both wings. Black's knight must maintain its guard duty, preventing the white h-pawn from advancing. The knight is thus unable to take part in the play on the other side of the board. The game continued **1.Kd3 Ke5 2.Ba8 Kd6 3.Kc4 g4 4.a4** (White's plan is to walk into a6 with his king, then capture on a7. Before doing so, however, he pushes his own a-pawn.) **4...Ng8 5.a5 Nh6 6.Be4 g3 7.Kb5 Ng8 8.Bb1 Nh6 9.Ka6 Kc6 10.Ba2 resigns.** After 10...Kc7 11.Kxa7 Kc6 12.Bc4 Kc7 13.Bd5, White can meet 13...Kd6 with 14.Kb6 Kxd5 15.a6, when nothing can stop the a-pawn, while 13...Nf5 loses simply to 14.Ka6 followed by Kb5.

Despite the fact that there was nothing on a white square for the bishop to attack, its influence was enough to lead to a win for White despite the reduced material. With the h-pawn tying down the knight in the diagram position, White is effectively playing with an extra piece on the other wing and even though he has only one pawn over there, it is enough to win.

This endgame should also serve as an example of the subtlety sometimes needed to judge apparently simple endgames. Bishop and three pawns against knight and three pawns hardly sounds very promising in terms of winning potential, yet White won this position without much difficulty.

pawn to rook three

In the days before women learnt to play chess, the Czech grandmasters used to call them 'little ears' – the pawns that timid lady players used to nudge to a3 and h3 as White, or a6 and h6 as Black*. After losing games as Black to a quick attack with e4, Bc4, Nf3 and Ng5, or being inconvenienced by having a knight pinned by a bishop, it seems sensible to deny your opponent a square in your half of the board by playing a harmless pawn move. And it comes in useful later on to avoid back-rank mates when you've castled. But how can you tell, so early in the game, whether you really want your pawn on that square?

> Pawn moves are the most difficult – they cannot move backwards.

Every time you advance a pawn, it increases your control of certain squares, but leaves permanent weaknesses behind it, however imperceptible they may seem. When you find yourself thinking about playing h6, or a similar defensive pawn nudge, ask yourself whether there isn't something more useful for you to be doing. Here are the circumstances that justify prodding a rook's pawn one square forwards.

- In order to drive back an enemy piece that has already ventured into your half of the board. Here the pawn move gains time rather than losing it.
- To prevent a bishop pinning a knight, *when that bishop has no other good square to develop to*. The pawn move then has a valuable cramping effect.
- When the pawn move itself forms part of a grand strategic plan – perhaps to support a later advance of its neighbour, or simply to avoid the exchange of a valuable bishop by giving it a bolt hole.
- When it is essential, for tactical reasons, to deny a square to the enemy knight or bishop.

*Timid men players do the same thing, but the grandmasters were rarely so rude about them.

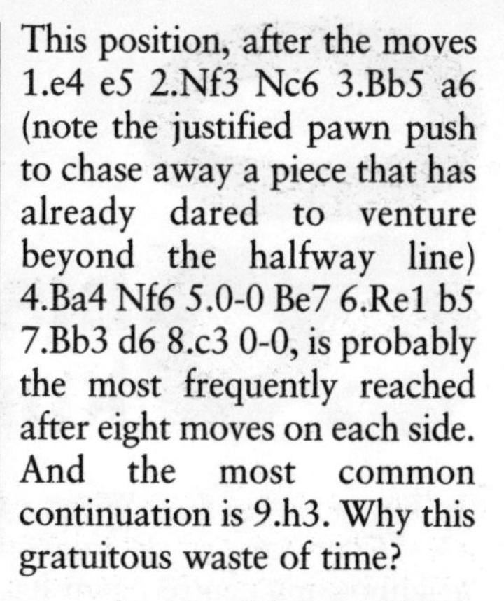

This position, after the moves 1.e4 e5 2.Nf3 Nc6 3.Bb5 a6 (note the justified pawn push to chase away a piece that has already dared to venture beyond the halfway line) 4.Ba4 Nf6 5.0-0 Be7 6.Re1 b5 7.Bb3 d6 8.c3 0-0, is probably the most frequently reached after eight moves on each side. And the most common continuation is 9.h3. Why this gratuitous waste of time?

White's pawn on c3 is supporting an advance of its neighbour to d4. The rook on e1 is not only defending the e-pawn, but lurking, ready to attack e5 if Black should advance his own d-pawn and allow exd5. So White is ready to gain the small advantage of pawns at d4 and e4 against pawns at d6 and e5.

After 9.d4 Bg4, however, it is difficult for White to hold his position in the centre. The threat is 10...exd4 11.cxd4 Bxf3, winning a pawn after 12.Qxf3 Nxd4, or causing weaknesses after 12.gxf3. Supporting the centre with 10.Be3 also interferes with the rook's action on the e-file while also inviting Black's knight to hop to a5 and c4. Finally, 10.d5 is not really in line with White's central strategy and encourages Black to nibble away at the formation with 10...Na5 11.Bc2 c6.

After 9.h3, however, the black bishop, though able to develop on d7, b7 or e6 (but ask yourself, before playing the last of these, whether you really want to exchange your white-squared bishop when your central pawns are on black squares) cannot take such an active role in the fight for the centre. White will, next move, secure his objective of securing the perfect centre of pawns on d4 and e4.

Interestingly enough, the move 9...h6 used to be a popular reply to 9.h3, with Black planning to continue with Re8, Bf8, g6 and Bg7, but fearing that 9...Re8 immediately would be met by 10.Ng5 with an annoying attack on f7. More recently, Black's most popular continuation has been 9...Bb7 10.d4 Re8, ready to meet 11.Ng5 with 11...Rf8, regaining the time lost by kicking the knight away with ...h6 next move.

08 bishop to knight's five

To pin or not to pin? When a knight makes its first move to f3, c3, f6 or c6, as it does more often than not, and the neighbouring centre pawn has also been moved, there is often the possibility to immobilize the knight by pinning it to the king or queen with a bishop. It's always pleasant to move into your opponent's half of the board especially when you immediately cut down his options by doing so. Yet the bishop-to-knight's-five pinning move is not always a good idea. For simplicity of notation, we'll discuss the case of White's Bg5 pinning a knight on f6 – though the comments apply equally to a black bishop on g4 or bishops on the other side of the board on b5 or b4.

First of all, you must ask yourself: 'What am I going to do if the bishop is attacked by a pawn moving to h6?' It's surprising how frequently you see club players moving a bishop to g5 with little hesitation, then sinking into deep thought when their opponent replies with h6. Knowing what you are going to do after h6 must be part of the decision to play Bg5.

> Always know your own intentions before your opponent forces you to reveal them.

There are several sets of circumstances that may make Bg5 a good move.

- When your opponent has already castled and chasing your bishop away with h6 and g5 would create too many weaknesses.
- When you have decided, in any case, that it is a good idea to exchange your bishop for a knight.
- When you plan to meet h6 by retreating the bishop on the c1–g5 diagonal and the pawn on h6 becomes a potential weakness later.
- When you still have a rook on h1, enabling h6 to be met by h4, when accepting the piece sacrifice would leave the king vulnerable to a mating attack down the newly opened h-file.

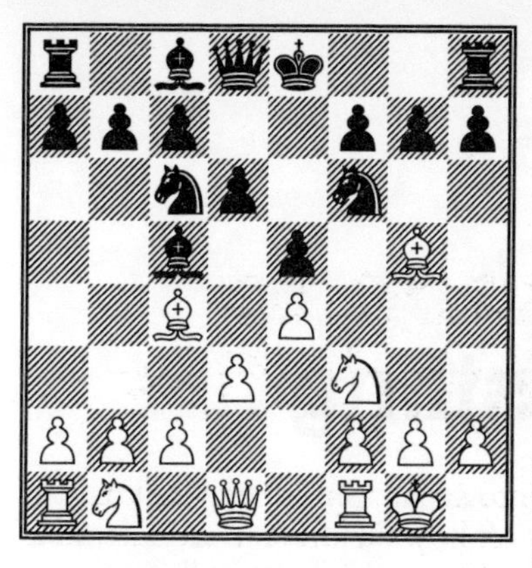

A cautionary tale of a blunt pin. This position was reached in the game Dubois-Steinitz, London 1861, after the moves **1.e4 e5 2.Nf3 Nc6 3.Bc4 Bc5 4.0-0 Nf6 5.d3 d6 6.Bg5.**

If Black had already castled, the pin might well be strong, but in this position it is totally misconceived. Here's how play continued.

6...h6 7.Bh4 g5! (Had Black castled, this move could even be met by 8.Nxg5!? hxg5 9.Bxg5 maintaining the pin and wrecking the black king's defences.) **8.Bg3 h5! 9.h4** (After 9.Nxg5, Steinitz gives the following entertaining possibility: 9...h4! 10.Nxf7 hxg3 11.Nxd8 Bg4 12.Qd2 Nd4 13.Nc3 Nf3+! 14.gxf3 Bxf3 15.Rd1 gxh2+ 16.Kf1 h1=Q mate.) **9...Bg4** (Now here's a pin with everything going for it – the bishop cannot even be chased by h3.) **10.c3** (10.hxg5 is again strongly met by h4.) **10...Qd7 11.d4 exd4 12.e5 dxe5 13.Bxe5 Nxe5 14.Nxe5** (White's imaginative central breakthrough has enabled him to escape from the pin, but his troubles are not over.) **14...Qf5 15.Nxg4 hxg4 16.Bd3 Qd5 17.b4 0-0-0!** (Confident that his attack must win the game, Black gives up a piece to get his king into safety.) **18.c4 Qc6 19.bxc5 Rxh4 20.f3 Rdh8 21.fxg4 Qe8 22.Qe1 Qe3+! 23.Qxe3 dxe3 24.g3** (The only defence to Rh1 mate.) **24...Rh1+ 25.Kg2 R8h2+ 26.Kf3 Rxf1+ 27.Bxf1 Rf2+ 28.Kxe3 Rxf1 29.a4 Kd7 30.Kd3 Nxg4 31.Kc3 Ne3 32.Ra2** (Desperation, but 32.Kb3 g4 33.Kb2 Nxc4+ or 33.Ka2 Nc2 would have been no better.) **32...Rxb1 33.Rd2+ Kc6 34.Re2 Rc1+ 35.Kd2 Rc2+ 36.Kxe3 Rxe2+ 37.Kxe2 f5 38.Ke3 Kxc5 39.Kd3 f4** and White finally resigned!

Had White thought a little longer after 6...h6, he would surely have captured the knight rather than retreat the bishop. Had he thought at all before 6.Bg5, he would surely have played something else entirely. After 6...h6 7.Bh4 g5 8.Bg3, Black does not even have to play imaginatively to gain the advantage. A simple plan of Qe7, Be6 and 0-0-0 would leave him well placed for a K-side attack, with the pawns well advanced on that wing and the bishop on g3 only getting in White's way.

castling

Castle early to get your king into safety, they always tell us, but we've just seen an example of how White ran into trouble precisely because he had castled early. While it is all to easy to run into trouble through leaving your king in the centre too long, there is a good deal to be said for delaying castling, if only to keep your opponent guessing and make it more difficult for him to formulate a precise attacking plan.

There are two good reasons for castling:

- because lines in the centre are open, or likely to become so in the near future, and the place is simply becoming too hot for a king;
- to connect the rooks and bring one ready to occupy a central file.

But if your rook is doing a good job on its original square – supporting an advance of an edge pawn or glaring down an open file at the enemy king – it may sometimes make more sense to leave it where it is and not castle at all.

> Castling is not just a king move.

When the centre of the board is safe, it can be good strategy to leave the king there until the moment comes for the cornered rook to play a part in the game. Some very strong players even show a marked reluctance to castle, always looking, before doing so, to see if there is a more active way to seize some advantage before tucking the king up in bed. If you adopt such a strategy, however, you have to work a little harder just to ensure that you are not taken by surprise by a sudden central breakthrough.

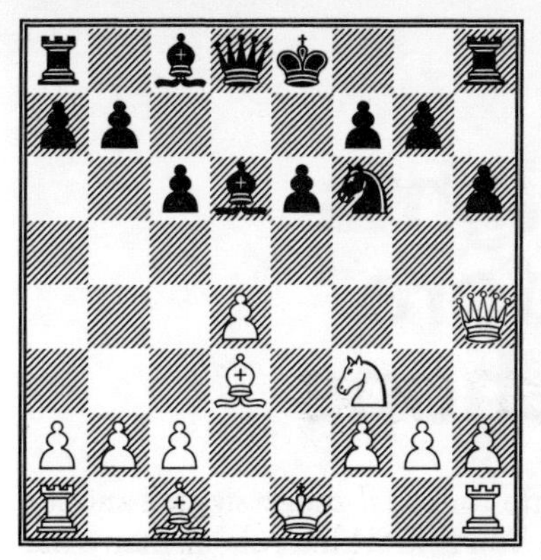

From the game Kamsky–Karpov, Dortmund 1993. It is Black to play. What should he be thinking of doing with his king?

There seem to be two main options: to castle K-side and brave the possible attack, or to prepare Q-side castling with Qc7, b6 and Bb7. Note, incidentally, how White has kept his own options of castling on either wing open. Particularly in the event of Black's castling K-side, it could be tempting for White to play Bd2 and 0-0-0, then attack with g4 and g5 to exploit the weakness caused by pushing the pawn to h6.

Black actually solved his problems in a surprising way. By playing **1...Ke7!** He renounced the right to castle and pinned his own knight, but the point of the move is that it provides his rook on h8 with a defender – the queen – and thereby creates the threat of 2...g5! when 3.Qh3 will run into trouble after ...g4 or ...e5. Suddenly, the emphasis of the position shifts from the insecurity of Black's king to the lack of squares available to White's queen. Rather than let himself be chased around after 2.Nd2 g5 3.Qh3 e5 4.Qe3 Nd5, Kamsky sacrificed a pawn with **2.Ne5!? Bxe5 3.dxe5 Qa5+ 4.c3 Qxe5+ 5.Be3**, but Black defended himself well and eventually won the game.

To advance boldly with 1...Ke7 in such a position is an extremely unusual idea, but worth remembering for two reasons: firstly, as a striking example of the fact that you do not always have to castle – just moving the king may occasionally be better; secondly, to remind yourself that the same applies to your opponent.

Finally, we should not leave this position before thinking about what would have happened had Black meekly castled. After 1...0-0, we have already mentioned the idea of Bd2, 0-0-0, g4 and g5. White has an even more dangerous possibility, however, in 2.Bxh6 gxh6 3.Qxh6. The threats of Bg5 or Ng5 followed by Bh7+ give every prospect of a quick mating attack. Another example of the dangers of an early ...h6 – if you don't follow it up correctly.

A deeper discussion of this position will be found in Section **62. Crime and Punishment.**

10 knights before bishops

It sounds like a rule of etiquette for royal processions – and it's about as much practical use. You'll find this rule in many old beginners' books as a piece of advice on the order in which you should bring out your pieces in the opening. It made some sense in the days when most games began 1.e4 e5 – you knew that the knights were going to end up on f3, f6, c3 and c6, but it made sense to delay development of the bishops. Where, for example, will Black's f8-bishop go? If White contents himself with a later d3, it should be looking for an active posting on c5; if White plays Nc3 and d4 too quickly, it might well venture to b4, but if White slowly prepares c3 and d4, perhaps the bishop should stay out of the way on e7 or g7.

The 'knights before bishops' nonsense is a specific case of a much more sensible piece of advice on development:

> Play the obvious before the optional.

In other words, keep your options open by playing the moves that have a certain place in your development scheme before taking decisions between the optional extras. Any decent development plan is bound to have a certain amount of inbuilt flexibility, to cope with various possibilities of the opponent. By maintaining that flexibility for as long as possible, you make it more difficult for your opponent to find the best squares for his pieces.

In many modern openings, that may even lead to a reversal of the 'knights before bishops' principle, even as early as the second move. For example, after the opening moves 1.c4 e5, White may opt for a plan of dominating the central white squares. For this, he will need his bishop on g2, which is a far higher priority than deciding where the knight on g1 will go. So 2.g3 Nc6 3.Bg2 is a logical continuation, leaving until later the decision whether to play Nf3, or e3 and Ne2, or even Nh3.

White to play – how should he plan to complete his development?

The great Estonian grandmaster Paul Keres used to score well from this position with White, using the trick of maintaining flexibility. The main question is: where should White move his b1-knight?

Think first about what is going to happen in the centre. White is unlikely to want to play cxd5, because that would bring a black knight to a powerful central square and leave White with an isolated d-pawn. That leaves two possibilities: Black will play dxc4 – in which case White will recapture with the pawn, leaving his pawns mobile (though the pawn on c4 may require some extra protection) – or White will eventually push c5.

Now look at the position from Black's point of view. He doesn't want to play dxc4 too soon, because after bxc4 he'll always have to worry about White's d5 advance, opening the long diagonal for the bishop on b2. But if he leaves the pawns as they are, he will have to keep an eye on White's plan of advancing c5, then continuing with b4 and a general Q-side advance. He can hold up c5 by putting the knight on d7, but there's a good deal to be said for having the knight on c6 in order to play Rc8, dxc4 and Na5 with good pressure against White's c-pawn.

All that explains why Keres always played 1.Qe2! in this position, meeting 1...Nc6 with 2.Nbd2!, giving an extra guard to c4 and planning to push Q-side pawns later with Rac1, c5, a3 and b4; while if Black played 1...Nbd7, he would continue 2.Nc3!, continuing with Rad1, Rfe1, Ne5 and f4, planning an attack in the centre and on the K-side. White's queen on e2 fits in well with either plan, so is the most flexible move in the position.

4 developing your pieces

First they tell you not to move each piece more than once in the opening, then they introduce you to the main line of the Ruy Lopez, in which White moves his bishop four times, ending up with it tucked away on c2, doing nothing active at all. What's it all about?

Your aim in the opening should be to get your pieces into play as quickly as possible, so that they can co-operate with one another, rather than getting in each other's way, and assist the more important plan of conquering territory and gaining space. If a piece takes more than one move to reach its most effective square, then so be it. What is important is to avoid wasting time. Don't move a piece to one square then change your mind next move and put it on another. While it is generally inadvisable to let your opponent gain time by chasing your pieces around the board, there is nothing wrong with letting them be chased if the chasing moves are non-developing ones. The important thing is this:

Nothing wastes time like time-wasting.

What is a waste of time is to spend two moves doing something that could have been accomplished in one, *while your opponent has made two useful moves in reply*. Every move in the opening should play its part in a grand design. Some of those moves will be positive – getting on with the task of bringing the pieces into play; some will be negative – solely designed to frustrate the opponent's aims; and some will be provocative – designed to tempt a weakening reply. But when the middlegame is reached, everything should be seen to have fitted together in a co-ordinated way. Nothing pointless and no waste of time.

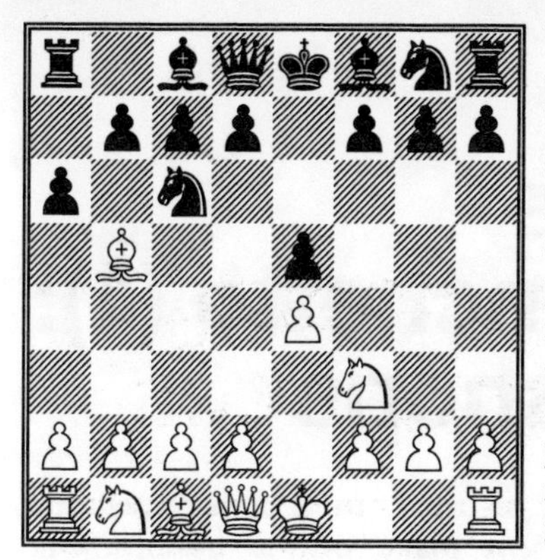

You have probably seen this position before. It's what happens when the most common White opening – the Ruy Lopez – is met by the standard reply 3...a6. Most players will now continue by rote either with 4.Bxc6 or 4.Ba4. Now is your chance actually to think about the position. What are the relative merits of the following continuations:

a) 4.Bxc6 dxc6 5.0-0; b) 4.Ba4 b5 5.Bb3; c) 4.Bc4?

The last of these can probably be dismissed as a waste of time. The word 'probably' has to qualify our assessment, however, because we ought to ask ourselves what difference it makes for the black pawn to be on a6 rather than a7. From Black's point of view it may be an advantage, since it could support a later advance of the b-pawn to b5, while any prospect that the pawn could be a weakness on a6 seems too distant to be worth taking into consideration.

4.Bxc6 dxc6 5.0-0 exchanges Black's sole developed piece, doubles his c-pawns and leaves White with a lead in development. The question is whether White is going to be able to do anything useful in the three moves it takes Black to castle. The exchange also leaves Black with a pair of bishops in the sort of open position in which bishops could well turn out to be better than knights. A lead in development can disappear, but a pair of bishops may be forever.

Finally, we come to 4.Ba4 b5 5.Bb3. White's bishop on b3 looks at first sight no better placed than it would have been on c4 at move three. There are, however, two very subtle points to appreciate. First, the bishop is actually more cosy on b3 than c4, because it is not liable to sudden attack by d5. Secondly, the pawn at b5 may become the target of attack by a4. If it then advances to b4, it leaves a nice square on c4 for White's pieces; if it captures on a4, it leaves an isolated a-pawn; if it stands its ground and allows axb5 to be played, it still leaves a vulnerable pawn on b5 as well as possibly ceding control of the a-file. White's bishop has indeed spent three moves getting to b3 instead of just two, but his intention is to prove that the pawn simply does not belong on b5.

2 the fianchetto (1): bishops

Imagine showing the rules of chess to a hyper-intelligent android. What would he/she/it make of the bishops? One possible hyper-intelligent line of thought might be as follows: bishops operate on diagonals. Every square on the board has two diagonals going through it, so every bishop is simultaneously operating in two directions. Every bishop, therefore, has one major diagonal and one minor one, and it makes sense to ensure that the major one is as long as possible. Conclusion: bishops are best deployed on the longest diagonals – the ones from corner to corner.

> Bishops are happiest on the long diagonals.

So after thinking for a long time over its first move, the android proudly plays 1.g3! just to make sure it gets its bishop to g2 before the opponent's bishop lands on b7. Having decided on 1.g3, it will also, no doubt, appreciate the defensive value of the formation with king castled behind a bishop on g2 and knight on f3, and it will also surely see the benefit of playing a pawn to c4, and perhaps even formulate the plan of advancing its neighbour to b4 and b5, just to enhance the bishop's influence on the long diagonal.

With one piece of logical thought, our android has invented the Réti Opening and laid the foundations for hypermodernism.

Some players have a straight up-and-down attacking style. Others take a sideways approach of cautious shuffling and probing. The diagonal players seek the best of both worlds: their bishops look forwards in attack, while glancing backwards in defence; instead of seeking eye-to-eye confrontation down open files, they peer askance down the diagonals, edging forwards and sideways, square by square, with the fianchettoed* bishop marshalling the troops from the rear.

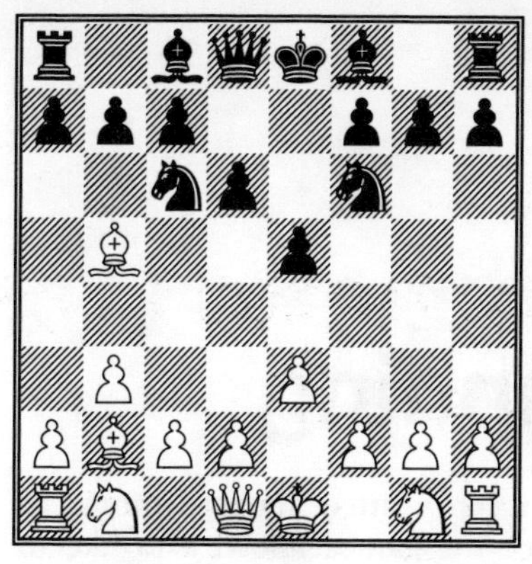

The Danish grandmaster Bent Larsen had great success in the early 1970s with the opening move 1.b3. This position was reached after four moves of his game against Brian Eley at Hastings 1972–3. How should White plan his next few moves to give his fianchettoed bishop the life it deserves?

The way Larsen chose was admirably logical: with the bishop on b2 at present limited in action by the black e-pawn, his first priority was to remove the blockage on its diagonal. He continued **5.Ne2 Bd7 6.0-0 Be7 7.f4! e4**. The next task is to give it some support: **8.Ng3** (In place to support a later attack on g7 with Nf5 or Nh5.) **8...0-0 9.Bxc6 bxc6 10.c4 d5 11.Nc3** (Don't worry that the bishop's view is impeded. It's only temporary.) **11...Re8 12.Rc1 Bg4 13.Nce2 Nd7** (Black has the sensible aim of challenging White's long diagonal control with Bf6. Somehow, though, he never gets round to it.) **14.h3 Bxe2 15.Qxe2 Nc5?** (Succumbing to a tempting beckon from the d3 square, but this was his last chance to play Bf6.) **16.Qg4 g6 17.f5! Nd3 18.fxg6 hxg6** (The power of the bishop is perfectly demonstrated after 18...fxg6 19.Qe6 mate.) **19.Rxf7! Kxf7** (19...Nxc1 or Nxb2 would have allowed mate in two with Qxg6+.) **20.Rf1+ Bf6** (or 20...Kg8 21.Qxg6 mate) **21.Bxf6 resigns**. The final position is worse than it looks: 21...Qc8 22.Be5+ Ke7 23.Qg5+ leads to a quick mate (23...Ke6 24.Qxg6+ Kxe5 25.Qf6+ is one pretty line), while 21...Qxf6 22.Qd7+! Re7 23.Rxf6+ Kxf6 24.Qxc6+ picks off the rook in the corner. Eley resigned at the correct moment: it was appropriate that the white bishop should have the last word.

*Strictly speaking, *fianchetto* is a noun – a diminutive of an Italian word meaning wing or flank – but the English have long misused it as a verb. The true pedant, however, will always refer to a 'bishop in fianchetto', and never a 'fianchettoed bishop'.

13 planning

Probably more nonsense has been written about planning in chess than any other aspect of the game. Those who like to imagine a moral dimension to chess strategy tell us that the game is won by the player who formulates a plan and carries it through properly. The worst sin, they say, is not to have a plan at all, but simply to lurch from move to move, reacting to circumstances rather than dictating events.

In fact, as many games are lost through pursuing bad plans as are won by pursuing good ones. One of the most effective strategies – especially at club level – is to wait for the opponent to have an idea, then show him what is wrong with it. In most positions, there is no such thing as a correct plan, only a flexible set of options ready to put into operation according to the options selected by the opponent.

The nearest you can come to the formulation of the plan is to ask yourself one simple question:

> Where would I like to see my pieces in five or six moves' time?

When you have calculated all the threats and captures in a position, and satisfied yourself that there is nothing you can do to win the game immediately, nor any defensive task that demands immediate attention, that's the question to ask. You then play a move that takes you nearer your ideal, half-a-dozen moves hence, position.

Your opponent's reply may put a spanner in the works and make you redesign your ideal formation, but two players impeding each other's plans is what good chess is all about. And the first time you actually succeed in carrying out all the moves of your blueprint, and then win the game by direct attack shortly after, you will feel a mixture of astonishment that your opponent didn't see it coming and pride that you have finally carried out a plan in the manner expected of you.

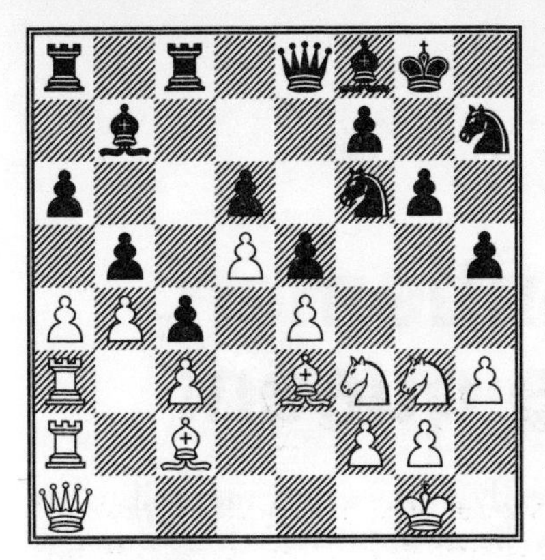

White to play; what's the plan?

The position comes from the first game of the 1992 rematch between Bobby Fischer (White) and Boris Spassky. It was Fischer's first serious game for 20 years, but his next few moves showed that his skills had not deserted him.

With his rooks and queen lined up on the a-file, it is clearly White's intention to unleash their power with axb5, but it pays to delay such a move. After all, Black is hardly going to play bxa4 willingly, since it will disrupt his own pawn formation and leave his pawns on c4 and a6 difficult to defend. With an exchange on b5 in the air, however, Black needs three men defending the rook on a8, so his bishop is tied to b7 and his queen to the back rank.

Fischer decided that what the position called for was a white piece poised to attack b5 after the pawn exchange on that square. Reasoning that his knight on g3 was not doing much at present, he formulated the plan of trotting it over towards a3. From the diagram, play continued: **1.Nf1! Be7 2.N1d2 Kg7 3.Nb1!** and Black is suddenly in real difficulties. The threat is 4.axb5 axb5 5.Rxa8 Rxa8 6.Rxa8 Qxa8 7.Qxa8 Bxa8 8.Na3 and the b-pawn cannot be defended. In other variations, a white rook or queen may come to a5 to help the attack against b5. Rather than wait passively, Spassky gave up a piece with **3...Nxe4 4.Bxe4 f5 5.Bc2 Bxd5,** but still did not succeed in saving the game.

Fischer's play from the diagram was surprising, but very logical. All White has to do is ask himself: 'Where would I like my pieces to be in a few moves time?' The single factor that would most improve White's game is to have a piece capable of attacking b5. Once you've had that idea, and realized that there's not much Black can do to improve his own game, the plan of Nf1, Nd2 and Nb1 ought not to be too difficult to formulate.

4 gentlemen, the queen!

Don't bring your queen out early in the game, they tell us, as though it were a crime against good etiquette. Yet the queen is the strongest piece, and from a central square can influence more of the board than any other. So what's wrong with putting her there?

The trouble is that a queen, when attacked by a lesser man – which, of course, covers everything other than another queen – has to run away. That's not just a problem for queens: no piece dare stand its ground when prodded by a man of lower value. Paradoxically a pawn controls territory better than any other man: when a pawn attacks a square, nothing dare tread there; if a queen attacks a square, anything except a king can happily stand there as long as it is protected.

The power of any piece to gain control of a square is inversely proportional to its value as a fighting piece.

That's what Philidor was driving at when he described the pawn as 'the soul of chess'. It's the pawns, not the queens, that play the most important role in the fight for space on the board. Every beginner finds it tempting to rush out with the queen and use her powers to attack in every direction, but if such attacks can be met by developing – or at least non-weakening – moves, then the queen's adventurousness is bound to end in loss of time when she is chased back.

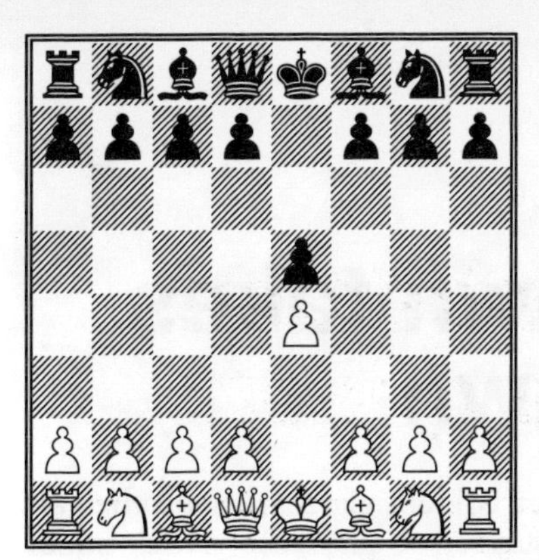

A surprisingly interesting position. After the moves 1.e4 e5, what is the difference between 2.d4 exd4 3.Qxd4 and 2.Nf3 Nc6 3.d4 exd4 4.Nxd4 Nxd4 5.Qxd4? If you appreciate the answer to that, you understand all you need to know about premature queen development.

The point is that after 2.d4 exd4 3.Qxd4, White's queen is exposed to attack by 3...Nc6 – a natural developing move, completely in keeping with Black's developing plan. After 4.Qe3 or 4.Qa4, there is nothing much wrong with White's game; he did, after all, move first, so he can afford to lose a move, but Black already leads the development race.

In the second continuation from the diagram, however, after 2.Nf3 Nc6 3.d4 exd4 4.Nxd4, Black's 4...Nxd4 is frequently criticized for 'bringing White's queen to a powerful post in the centre'. After 5.Qxd4, Black can attack the queen with 5...c5, but that is not only a non-developing move, it even loses control for ever over the d5 square. 5...Ne7 followed by 6...Nc6 would be a rather better way of annoying her majesty, but that takes two moves to get the knight developed when it really ought to find a decent square in one.

In the first variation, after 3.Qxd4, White's queen is exposed to attack on d4 and immediately forced to waste time; in the second variation, her influence from the central square is a genuine irritant to Black's smooth development. Her attack on g7 makes it difficult for the bishop to move from f8, and she can only be chased from d4 at the cost of time-wasting or creating weaknesses. For a queen, the difference between premature development and powerful centralization can be very small indeed.

pawn takes pawn

When two pawns of different colours glare at each other on neighbouring diagonal squares, it is rarely an equal relationship. The tension created by the possibility of an exchange of pawns tends to favour one side or the other. Usually the decision to resolve that tension rests predominantly with one player, who can exploit the situation by keeping the tension as long as possible.

> Pawn takes pawn is never a fair exchange.

Imagine the central pawn position that arises in many king's pawn openings with white pawns at c3, d4 and e4 against black pawns at c7, d6 and e5. There are three ways the situation can be resolved: (1) Black plays exd4; (2) White plays dxe5; (3) White pushes forwards with d5.

In the first case, White most naturally responds with cxd4, leaving him with pawns at e4 and d4 against a pawn at d6. All other things being equal (which, of course, they never are), this will convey a large advantage through better central control.

In the second case, Black may recapture with dxe5, leaving an almost symmetrical pawn position. In the third, the nature of the position is changed radically, turning from a dynamic potentially open game into a relatively blocked one with a closed centre. Since Black's exd4 is a concession, it pays White to keep the tension and maintain the option to exchange or block.

Another example is when one side is trying to open a rook's file against a king castled behind a fianchetto. Typically, Black plays g6, Bg7 and 0-0; White barges ahead with h4 and h5. Since Black will be unlikely to risk wrecking his king's protective pawn shield by playing gxh5, White has the choice of when to relax the tension with hxg6 or even h6. The only advantage of playing hxg6 quickly is to force Black to decide whether he wants to recapture with f-pawn or h-pawn.

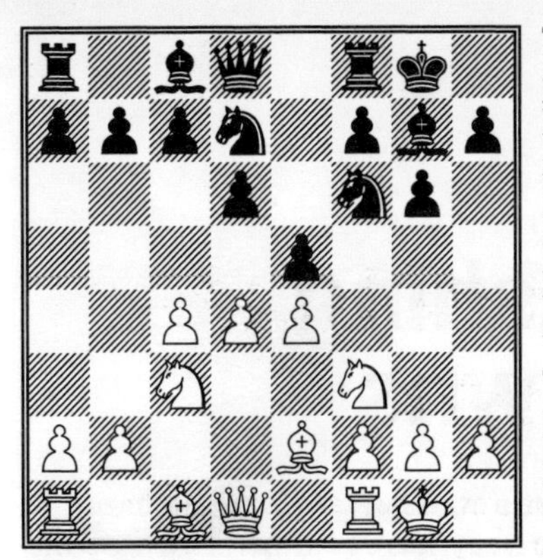

This is one of the main line positions in the King's Indian Defence (reached after the moves 1.d4 Nf6 2.c4 g6 3.Nc3 Bg7 4.e4 d6 5.Be2 0-0 6.Nf3 e5 7.0-0 Nbd7). How will the central tension resolve itself?

There are three possibilities: Black plays exd4, White plays dxe5, and White plays d5, and they all lead to very different types of game. If Black plays exd4, he cedes ground in the centre in exchange for an open diagonal for his bishop on g7, possible pressure on the e-file against the pawn on e4, and good squares at c5 and e5 for his knights.

If White plays dxe5, it leaves him with a weak square at d4, but some prospects of advancing on the Q-side with b4 and c5. If he plays d5, he must again look to advancing b4 and c5, with pressure against the Q-side. Black, meanwhile, will try to organize an advance on the opposite wing by moving his knight from f6 and playing f5.

In the early 1950s, several grandmaster games continued instructively with **8.Re1** (keeping all options open and ensuring that the rook can defend e4 if Black plays exd4 and Re8) **8...c6 9.Bf1 Re8 10.d5**.

Black has tried not to give away his plan too quickly, saving exd4 for the moment when he will be able to seize the initiative to compensate for his giving ground in the centre. White, however, has been waiting for the rook to move from f8 before pushing his pawn to d5. With the centre blocked, Black wants to play f5, which requires the support of a rook on f8.

After **10.d5**, play would often continue **10...c5** (though there is also a good deal to be said for Qe7 or Qc7, defending d6 and keeping open Black's option of cxd5 or c5) **11.a3** (preparing another favourable pawn confrontation with b4) **11...Rf8!?** putting the rook back where it now belongs.

White may claim to have tricked Black into losing two moves by his clever timing of d5. Black will stoutly maintain that his clever Re8 lured White into closing the centre, which is just the pre-condition needed for him to prepare to launch his K-side advance with f5.

6 pushing pawns

Pawns are insecure little creatures. They are at their happiest and most efficient only when they have another pawn of the same colour standing next to them. That simple truth lies at the basis of a vast amount of strategic play. Once you have opening 1.e4 as White, your principal aim is to find a way for the neighbouring pawn to move alongside it to d4, or if that proves impossible, then f4.

It's all very logical. Just look at the squares covered by a couple of pawns abreast: two pawns at d4 and e4 cover all of c5, d5, e5 and f5. If your opponent is denied the use of all those squares for his pieces, it can have serious consequences. Compare this with, for example, pawns at d4 and e5, which control c5, d6 and f6, and you will see the difference. The first creates a major obstacle for the opponent in the centre of the board; the second is merely a small collection of minor irritations.

When you have your pawns in the ideal, side-by-side formation, never push one without thinking about the friend it leaves behind. Especially in endgames, you should always be reluctant to advance such a pawn until you have a good idea of how its colleague will catch up.

> In endgames, advance your pawns two at a time.

Any pawn that advances leaves behind it squares that it will never again to able to control. And that, in all phases of the game, is the principle underlying any plan to increase one's control of space on the board.

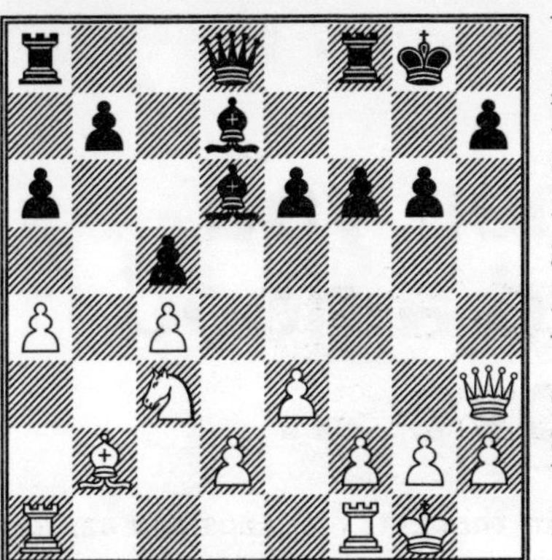

White to play and push his pawns. From the game Nimzowitsch–Michel, Semmering 1926, this is a remarkable example of a game won by a stampede of pawns.

With a pair of bishops and no obvious weaknesses, Black appears to stand well, yet White exposed the limitations of his position dramatically, winning the game in just eight more moves, of which seven were made with pawns.

The only problem with Black's position is a lack of good pawn moves. He does not want to play e5, because it gives away the d5 square to White's knight; he does not want to play f5, because it enhances the power of the bishop on b2. White can exploit this by pushing his own pawns:

1.f4! Qe7 2.e4!

Creating a huge weakness on d4 – but with no black knight to exploit it, the square is not weak at all.

2...Bc6 3.g4!

With three pawns abreast, White is now ready for anything. He may plan a later g5, to open the long diagonal for his bishop, or f5, to gain the d5 square for his knight, or e5 to push Black further backwards. Faced with this advancing army of pawns, Black decided to challenge them at once. It was a poor decision.

3...f5? 4.gxf5 exf5 5.e5 Bc7 6.Nd5! Bxd5 7.cxd5

With two pawns reunited side-by-side at the front of his formation, White threatens d6, winning a piece...

7...Qd7 8.e6

...or e6 winning the game. When Black's queen moves, White will play 9.Qc3, leaving Black helpless against the threat of mate on the long diagonal.

Black resigned.

when you find a good move ...

We have already seen that our thoughts on a position can be divided into the fuzzy and the precise. Fuzzy thought is the fumbling process of getting acquainted with the potential of a position by trying out likely looking possibilities; precise thought is the calculation of essential variations.

But when you've fumbled and analysed, and all the signposts point to one particular move, when is the moment to sign contracts and play it? The great German player Dr Siegbert Tarrasch advised: 'When you've found a good move, look for a better one.' What nonsense! When you've found a good move, play it! Good moves are few and far between. Don't talk yourself out of them. But make sure they are as good as you think.

There is a very useful rule for deciding on a restaurant in Paris: wander the streets until you find one restaurant you like; then go to the first one you see that is better. But it only works in Paris, or another city where there are many good restaurants. When looking for a good move in a chess position, it's like searching for a restaurant in some run-down holiday resort in England. Hence the practical rule for good moves:

When you've found a good move, savour it!

Strong players always think a good deal before playing 'obvious' winning moves. If it's really a winning move, you can even spare the time to look at every legal reply your opponent has at his disposal. And having tied up every loophole, you play the move with calmness and confidence.

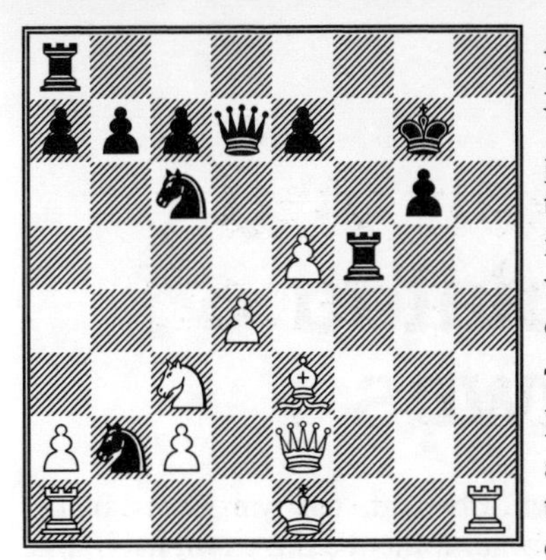

A complex tactical decision: Black threatens 1...Nxd4. Would you play: (a) **1.Qb5**, preventing Nxd4 and threatening Qxb2; (b) **1.d5**, intending to meet 1...Nxe5 with 2.Bd4; or (c) **something else?**

This position, from Gipslis–Botvinnik, Moscow 1965, is a highly complex example of the hazards of imprecise calculation. White's best move, according to Botvinnik, was 1.Qb5, hunting down the knight on b2. (Note that 1.Qh2 is met by Rh5!) Instead, the game continued (with How-Not-To-Think comments in italics) as follows:

1.d5

(This must be good: he must move the attacked knight, and after 1...Nxe5 2.Bd4, I calculate I'll win either the knight on e5 or the one on b2.)

1...Rxe5!

Now 2.dxc6 Qxc6 attacks both the rook on h1 and knight on c3. The only move to defend both is 3.Kd2 when 3...Nc4+ wins the bishop.

2.Bd4

He probably overlooked this. Now I stand much better. 2...Nxd4 loses to 3.Qxe5+, so he must defend his rook with 2...Qd6, when 3.Bxe5+ leaves White on top.

2...Nc4!

Apparently impossible, because the white queen controls that square. Note how the queen is pinned by a pinned rook. Such circumstances can easily create optical illusions in one's mental image of the position.

The game then continued **3.Bxe5+ N(3)xe5 4.Rh4 Rh8 5.Rxh8 Kxh8** when Black's active queen and beautifully positioned knights made White's game untenable. Botvinnik won after nine more moves. 1.d5 was not such a good move after all.

isolated pawns

As the great Aaron Nimzowitsch said, the weakness of an isolated pawn lies not in the vulnerability of the pawn itself, but in the weakness of the square in front of it. Well that's what he's often quoted as having said, but what he actually said was: '... it is not only the isolani itself that tends to become a weakness, but also the complex of squares surrounding it.'

An isolated pawn, should you need reminding, is one without a pawn of the same colour on a neighbouring file. So, unless a pawn capture is made, the isolated pawn cannot be defended by another pawn. In an endgame, a single isolated pawn may be a decisive weakness. By attacking it from all sides, the opponent may force a small army of pieces to be dedicated to its defence. Then, even if the pawn itself does not fall, a switch of direction by the attacking pieces may pose insoluble problems.

> An isolated pawn demands an aggressive policy.

For an isolated pawn and a defensive frame of mind add up only to trouble. So why do people willingly accept isolated pawns in the opening? The answer is usually a combination of space and freedom. To take an instant example: after the moves 1.d4 d5 2.c4 dxc4 3.e3 c5 4.Bxc4 cxd4 5.exd4, White has an isolated d-pawn. He hopes that its control of the e5 square will enable a knight to settle there and menace the opponent's K-side. Meanwhile, Black puts his faith in the d5 square, a safe central outpost for his own minor pieces. In the middle-game, White will have the initiative, thanks to the presence of his pawn on d4. His outpost square on e5 is, after all, in his opponent's half of the board. But if play reaches an endgame, when attacks on the king become less of a threat, the advantages of the isolated pawn may disappear, leaving it a weakness in need of constant defence.

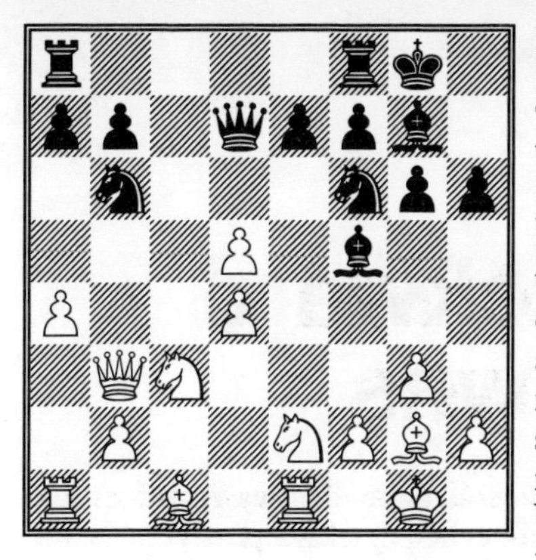

Black to play in Fuchs–Bronstein, East Berlin 1968. The battle here is over White's doubled, isolated d-pawns. Black, who is a pawn behind, plans to attack d5 with everything at his disposal, win back the pawn, and leave himself with a piece firmly entrenched on the square in front of White's remaining isolated pawn. White, in the meantime, must find something to do while Black is distracted by the task of regaining the pawn.

Black began with the natural **1...Rad8** which was met by **2.d6!** Now 2...exd6 would firstly give Black an isolated pawn of his own, secondly block the file on which Black wants to attack White's d-pawn, and thirdly invite the reply 3.a5, chasing the knight away and winning the b-pawn. Bronstein, however, was ready for this and played **2...Qxd6! 3.Nb5** (3.Bxb7 Rb8 gives Black plenty of activity) **3...Qd7!** (far better than 3...Qb8 4.Bf4 when Black is in a terrible mess) **4.Nxa7 Nbd5 5.Nb5 Be4.**

What has Black got for his pawn? A fine square in front of an isolated pawn is the answer. White should now play 6.f3, preserving his white-squared bishop even if it is rather boxed in. Instead White, in the knowledge that he was a pawn ahead, felt that he should not be averse to exchanging pieces. There followed **6.Nf4 Bxg2 7.Kxg2 b6 8.Qf3** (8.Nxd5 would have been more consistent) **8...Nb4! 9.Re2 Rfe8 10.Be3??** (a splendid blunder, completely missing the point of Black's play) **10...g5! 11.Nh5** (with the bishop in the way, d3 is no longer available) **11...g4! 12.Nxf6+ exf6 13.Qf4 Nd5!** And White resigned; his queen is trapped in mid-board. Never can the square in front of an isolated pawn have been so potent.

9 backward pawns

When a pawn is left behind its colleagues as they rush forward to attack, the poor laggard is called backward – yet it's the other pawns who have done the damage. If, for example, you play c4 and e4 as White, the d-pawn may be called backward. If it cannot catch up with the others because Black has a firm hold on the d4 square, then it suffers from the same vulnerability as an isolated pawn, since it will never be able to rely on its colleagues to defend it. Again, like an isolated pawn, it has one or more weak squares in front of it, but that is where the similarity ends. While its weaknesses may be similar to those of an isolated pawn, the potential strengths of a backward pawn are quite different.

A backward pawn is a liability when:

a it is vulnerable to attack; or
b an enemy piece may settle unmolested on the square in front of it.

A backward pawn is not a problem when:

a it can catch up with its colleagues; or
b the square in front of it can be adequately controlled.

A backward pawn may be an asset when:

a it controls an important central square; or
b it acts as a back support for an aggressively advancing phalanx of pawns.

> A backward pawn may act as a nurse to its companions.

So, in the example of White's playing e4 and c4, the backward d-pawn may sit on d3, like the fat man at the back of a tug-of-war team, as his colleagues expand with f4 and f5.

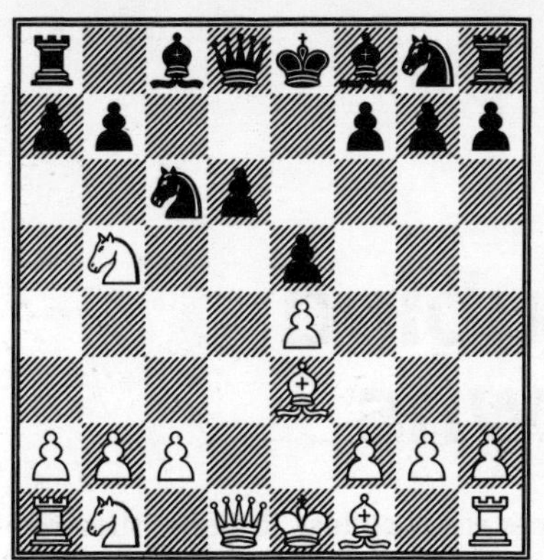

This position was reached in one of the games of the Morphy–Anderssen match in Paris in 1858 after the moves 1.e4 c5 2.d4 cxd4 3.Nf3 Nc6 4.Nxd4 e6 (creating a backward pawn on d7) 5.Nb5 (attracted like a moth to the glaring weakness on d6) 5...d6 6.Bf4 e5 7.Be3.

White's play has been remarkably sophisticated for a game from the mid-19th century. He has lost a move with his bishop, and moved his knight three times already (and will have to move it again if Black plays ... a6), all to create a firmly backward black d-pawn. But it will all be worthwhile if White can secure the unmolested use of the d5 square. The entire fight now should be over that square. Black should be thinking of moves such as Nf6 and Be6, ready to exchange anything that moves to d5; White will want a knight on c3 and, if given the opportunity, his bishop on c4. The other bishop may well move to g5 to exchange a knight on f6, thus increasing White's influence over d5 again. Anderssen, however, misunderstood the position and continued **7...f5?! 8.N1c3 f4?** (Fearing 8...a6 9.Nd5! axb5 10.Bb6 with Nc7+ to follow, he allows something far worse. The right move was 8...Nf6.) **9.Nd5! fxe3 10.Nbc7+ Kf7** (or 10...Kd7 11.Qg4 mate) **11.Qf3+ Nf6 12.Bc4 Nd4 13.Nxf6+ d5 14.Bxd5+ Kg6?** (Rather than enter an endgame a pawn behind with 14...Qxd5 15.Nxd5+ Nxf3+ 14.gxf3, he plays a move that loses immediately.) **15.Qh5+ Kxf6 16.fxe3!** (avoiding the little trap of 16.Ne8+? Qxe8 17.Qxe8 Bb4+) **16...Nxc2+** (16...Qxc7 17.exd4 leaves Black's king hopelessly exposed.) **17.Ke2 Black resigned.** 17...Qxc7 18.Rf1+Ke7 19.Rf7+ Kd6 20.Rxc7 Kxc7 21 Rc1 is hopeless for Black, while 17...Nxa1 leads to disaster after 18.Rf1+ Ke7 19.Qxe5+Kd7 20.Be6+Kc6 (or 20...Ke7 21.Rf1 mate) 21.Rc1+ with mate in at most two more moves.

20 doubled pawns

In the mathematics of geometrical solids, Euler's theorem connects the number of vertices, faces and edges of a solid by a simple formula: $V + F - E = 2$. So, for a cube, for example, there are eight vertices and six faces, so the number of edges, E, must equal $8 + 6 - 2$, which is 12. Absolutely correct. What has all this to do with doubled pawns? I'll tell you: $P + O - D = 8$

> Pawns plus Open Files minus Doubled Pawns equals Eight.

(Counting one for each pair of doubled pawns, or two for tripled pawns and so on.) Every doubled pawn gives you an extra open file for your rooks to play on. Not only that, but the pawns themselves, since they stand on the file adjacent to the open one, add to your ability to control the squares on the file.

That was the good news. The side-effects, however, are less desirable. There are three main defects of doubled pawns.

1. When you have two pawns on the same file, not only does the front one impede the advance of its colleague, but the pair, as they advance, control identical squares. The result must be an equivalent loss of control over other squares.
2. Doubled pawns can cripple a pawn majority. If you have more pawns on one wing than your opponent, you will normally be able to create a passed pawn. This may no longer be the case if your formation includes doubled pawns.
3. Doubled pawns cannot defend each other. This weakness is particularly accentuated in the case of doubled, isolated pawns.

As for tripled pawns and quadrupled pawns, all the above applies, only more so. There is, however, one last, totally unimportant point to be made about pawns stacked vertically: a player with sextupled pawns on the a-file or h-file can never lose. Why? Because it takes 15 captures to get them there, so the opponent can have only his king left.

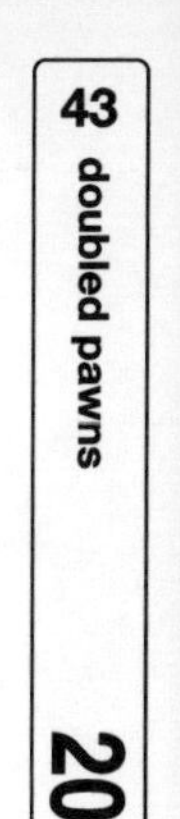

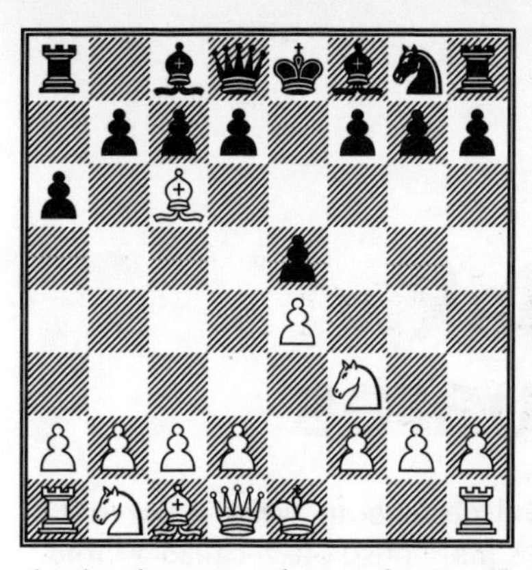

A tricky doubled-pawn problem for Black. Which way to recapture?

In this position from the Ruy Lopez, reached after the moves 1.e4 e5 2.Nf3 Nc6 3.Bb5 a6 4.Bxc6, most Black players take the bishop with the d-pawn without thinking. Yet few could provide any convincing justification for preferring dxc6 to bxc6. Indeed, it is almost easier to think of reasons for preferring the recapture with the b-pawn.

- It is generally better to capture towards the centre than away from it: 4...bxc6 leaves more black pawns able to fight for control of the central squares.
- Admittedly, after 4...dxc6 5.Nxe5 Black regains the pawn easily with 5...Qd4, but 4...bxc6 5.Nxe5 also looks not at all bad for Black after either 5...Qe7 or even 5...Qg5 6.Ng4 d5.
- After 4...dxc6, it is the easiest thing in the world for White to gain a structural advantage for the endgame: 5.d4 exd4 6.Qxd4 Qxd4 7.Nxd4 leaves White with a workable K-side pawn majority, while Black's majority on the other wing is crippled by the doubled pawns. Indeed, if all the pieces were then to be exchanged, Black's doubled pawns would lose the game for him.

Yet there are other factors to take into account, not least Black's bishop pair, which has more scope after 4...dxc6. Also, precise analysis shows that Black's game is not easy after 4...bxc6 5.Nc3 d6 6.d4 exd4 7.Qxd4. Whatever formation Black then adopts for his d-pawn and two c-pawns, he is liable to be left with weaknesses.

There is, however, one neat trap involving 4...bxc6 which has caught several players. After 5.d4 exd4 6.Qxd4 Qf6 7.e5 Qg6 8.0-0 (where most standard textbooks break off with the easy conclusion: 'White has a clear advantage'), Black plays 8...Bb7! If Black also puts on just the right expression of suppressed panic, White may be tempted into 9.e6 fxe6 10.Ne5, when his dreams of a quick victory are quashed by 10...Qxg2+! 11.Kxg2 c5+ with a winning position for Black.

2 weak squares

We have already talked a good deal about weak squares; it's time we defined them. A weak square (also often called a 'hole') is a square on your third or fourth rank which can never again be defended by one of your pawns. So if you play c4 and e4 as White, you are creating weak squares at both d3 and d4. Now you can see that a backward pawn is only a perfectly ordinary pawn sitting on a weak square. Only it's much easier to grasp the significance of a weak pawn than to understand the relevance of a weak square. When a pawn is weak, your opponent may attack it, win it and he's a pawn ahead. But what's so bad about losing a square?

The trouble is, when your opponent gains control of a square in your half of the board and has the opportunity to establish one of his pieces on it, the influence of that piece may be enough to cause the defences to crumble. The crucial element, however, is establishing a piece on the weak square. Any square that cannot be defended by a pawn may be said to be weak, but the weakness is only a defect if it provides an outpost that the opponent can use.

A weakness that cannot be exploited is not a weakness at all.

As pawns advance, they can hardly help but leave weak squares in their wake. Even the move 1.e4 leaves d3, d4, f3 and f4 a little less secure than they were. The whole art of pawn play lies in ensuring that no true weaknesses develop on the squares the pawns abandon. Ideally the pawns will move steadily forward, conquering space in a manner that does not allow the outflanking needed to get to the squares behind them. When this is not possible, one should at least ensure that important squares deprived of their pawn defenders are still capable of being defended by pieces.

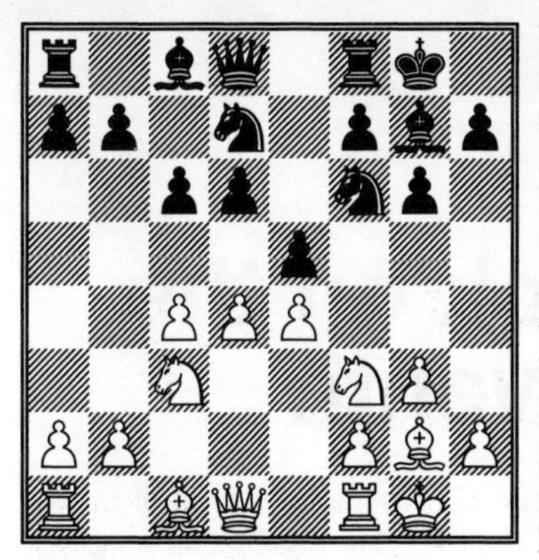

White to play and lose a square. This position from the King's Indian Defence is reached after the moves 1.d4 Nf6 2.c4 g6 3.g3 Bg7 4.Bg2 0-0 5.Nc3 d6 6.Nf3 Nbd7 7.0-0 e5 8.e4 c6. Three things can now happen to resolve the central tension: White may, at some stage, block the position by advancing d5; or Black may, at some moment, open the game with exd4; or White may exchange pawns himself with dxe5. One of these is inherently unfavourable to White. Which one?

Structurally speaking, White must, above all else, avoid the temptation to capture on e5. After 9.dxe5 dxe5, just look at the d4 square. There is no black piece within a mile of it at the moment, but once the exchange has been made, Black knows what he has to do and ideas such as Re8, Bf8 and Bc5, or Nc5 and Ne6, or Re8, Nf8 and Ne6 rush automatically to the front of the strategic brain. Eventually, a black bishop or knight established at d4 will create threats on both wings, or in the endgame a rook on d4 will give Black a commanding control of the d-file, or even, in a king and pawn endgame, a black king penetrating to d4 will win the game. White's best hope may be to capture any piece that arrives at d4, but even that will leave Black with a nicely supported passed pawn after the e-pawn recaptures.

The only thing that can justify White's dxe5 capture would be if he could himself quickly play c5, Nd2, Nc4 and Nd6, exploiting Black's own hole at d6, but even that is, on its own, an inferior option. After all, d4, being right in the centre, is a better square than d6 anyway.

Finally, look at the difference if White closes the centre with d5 instead of dxe5. He still has a weak square at d4 but, denied the use of c6 and e6, Black's knights will be hard pressed to get there. And his black-squared bishop is locked behind his pawns, and the d-file is closed, so the weak d4 square is not a weakness at all. On the other hand, the d5 advance also, by blocking the position, shields the weak pawn at d6 from attack after Black plays c5 in reply. In practice, therefore, White usually keeps his options open, playing neither d5 nor dxe5, but a developing move such as 9.Re1, awaiting events.

22 rook on the seventh

The 'rook on the seventh' is one of those handy catch-phrases – like 'close to local amenities' in an estate agent's catalogue – that brings an automatic smile to the face of the prospective purchaser. The seventh rank is the Mecca for rooks: in the middlegame, the rook on the seventh is the precursor to a mating attack; in the endgame it promises a rich harvest of pawns.

Yet while a rook on the seventh is a good thing more often than not, countless games have been lost through an unsupported rook's barging through to that destination, only to be chased away a few moves later with a ruinous loss of time. Those handy local amenities suddenly prove to be hostile after all.

There are two good things about a rook on the seventh: it may restrict the enemy king – either for attacking purposes or simply to prevent him taking an active role in the endgame – and it is best placed there to molest enemy pawns, either directly, because they have not yet moved, or by sneaking up behind them if they have. But in either case, there is little point in galloping all that way down the board if the rook is only going to be chased back again.

A rook needs room to stretch its wings.

Sometimes, you can slide your rook down to the seventh almost without thinking. Usually, however, it is worth pausing to ask yourself whether the rook can fulfil its mission, whether your other pieces can support its efforts, or whether it will be chased back before it has done any damage.

Those pawns that you thought your rook was attacking may also serve to deny it the room it needs. And sometimes, when your opponent's king has left the back rank and his pawns have mostly moved from their original squares, it's the rook on the *sixth* that will do the damage, not on the seventh at all.

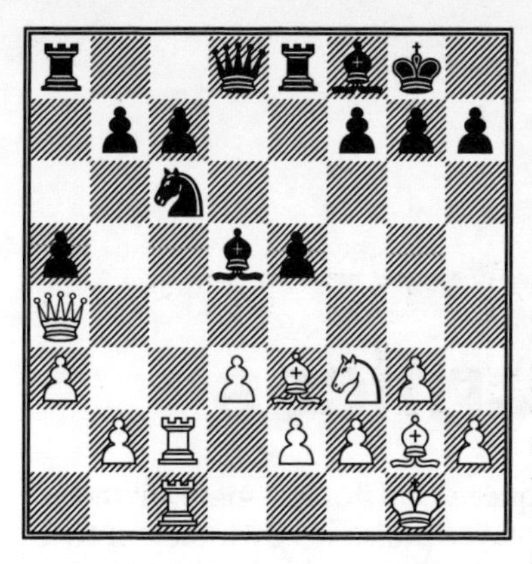

Botvinnik–Portisch, Monte Carlo 1968. This position, with Black to play, was the prelude to one of the greatest of all rooks on the seventh. As White's rooks on the c-file clearly signal, his plan is to put pressure on the knight on c6, then break through to the seventh rank. Portisch found a clever idea to try to negate the whole concept. He played **1...Nb8.** If White then takes on c7, Black cuts off the lines of communication with Bc6 and traps the rook on c7. If White does not take on c7, then Black simply plays c6, leaving the rooks biting on granite. Now look what happened after 1...Nb8:

2.Rxc7! Bc6 3.R1xc6! bxc6 4.Rxf7!!

The rook spreads its wings and nearly knocks Black's king over. After 4...Kxf7 5.Qc4+ Kg6 (Ke7 or Kf6 lose to Bg5+) 6.Qg4+ Kf7 7.Ng5+ every line leads to mate or win of the black queen. Portisch's next move denies g5 to the white knight and makes real the threat to take the rook.

4...h6 5.Rb7 Qc8 6.Qc4+ Kh8 7.Nh4!

The rook on the seventh has done its job and now gives its life.

7...Qxb7 8.Ng6+ Kh7 9.Be4! Bd6

The threat was 10.Ne7+ Kh8 11.Qg8 mate.

10.Nxe5+ g6 11.Bxg6+ Kg7 12.Bxh6+! resigns.

After 12...Kxh6 13.Qh4+ Kg7 14.Qh7+ Kf6 15.Ng4+ Ke6 (or 15...Kg5 16.Qh5 mate) 16.Qxb7, White wins comfortably.

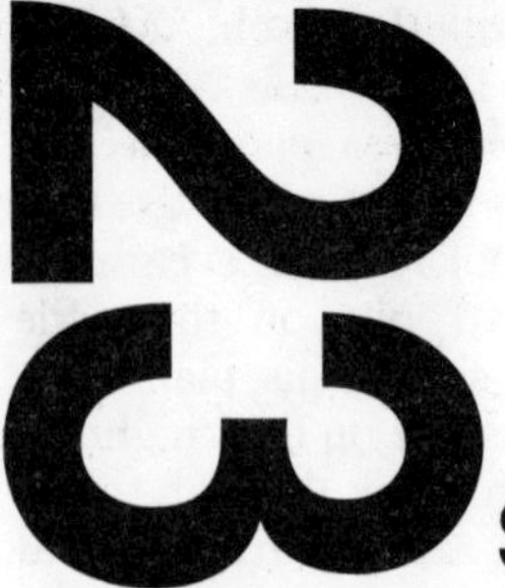

23 sacrifices

'...and then I sacrificed my queen and forced mate in three.' How often have you heard a player praise his own play in such a manner? Well I'm happy to disillusion him. That's not a sacrifice. How can giving up a mere queen in order to gain a king be called a sacrifice?

The sacrificial combination that leads to a forced win – or at least a forced advantage – should be part of any player's tactical technique. It's just a question of teaching yourself to overcome the mental blocks that exist against even considering any move that appears to lose material. We explained all that in **2. Calculation.**

The true sacrifice is a far nobler venture. It involves surrendering material for some long-term positional advantage. In practice, most genuine sacrifices fall into one of two categories:

1 A pawn sacrifice (known as a gambit) in the opening to gain time or central control.

2 The exchange sacrifice in the middlegame – giving up rook for knight or bishop – in order to crumple your opponent's pawns and create strong squares for your own minor pieces while the enemy rooks can play no effective role.

Sacrificing anything more than the exchange in return for intangible benefits is rare, except where there is a direct weakening of the opponent's king in a manner that promises a successful mating attack. In such cases, Capablanca's Rule may apply:

> If the potential attacking forces outnumber the available defenders, then the attack will win.

The questions are: how long will the attackers need to take up their aggressive positions, how long will it take them to carry out their mission after that, and will all that give the defence enough time to muster its reserves?

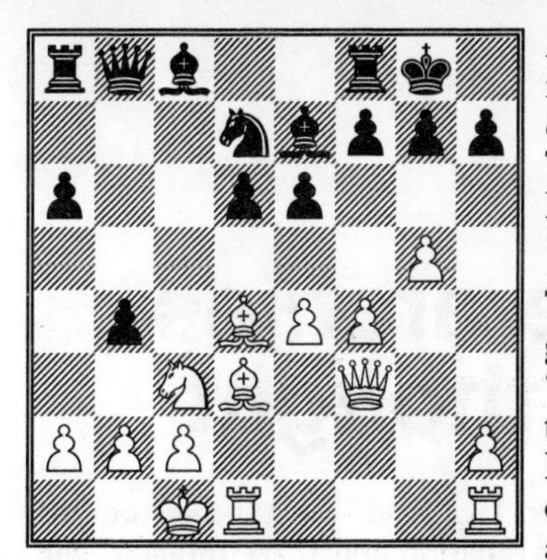

A genuine sacrifice from the final game of a world title qualifying match. Mikhail Tal, playing White against Bent Larsen in 1965, played **1.Nd5! exd5 2.exd5.**

Tal's commentary to the game explains everything: 'Black's pieces are grouped on the Q-side (Ra8, Qb8 and Bc8) and it is by no means easy for them to come to the aid of their king. The open e-file is a barrier.' He went on to explain that White already has a threat of launching a standard mating attack with 3.Bxh7+ Kxh7 4.Qh5+ Kg8 5.Bxg7 Kxg7 6.Qh6+ Kg8 7.g6 and Black must make further concessions to avoid this. Playing 2...g6 would invite 3.h4 followed by h5, when every white piece joins the attack. Larsen chose the other defence:

2...f5 3.Rde1 Rf7 4.h4 Bb7 5.Bxf5 Rxf5 6.Rxe7

Now if Black defends with 6...Rf7, he is quickly ripped apart by 7.Rxf7 Kxf7 8.g6+! hxg6 9.h5 when the attacking forces rush in with nothing to fight them off. Larsen decided to give back the piece to gain some activity.

6...Ne5 7.Qe4 Qf8! 8.fxe5 Rf4 9.Qe3

Now Black should play 9...Bxd5 when after 10.exd6! Rxd4 11.Qxd4 Bxh1 12.b3 all is still unclear. Instead, there followed 9...Rf3 10.Qe2 Qxe7 11.Qxf3 dxe5 12.Re1 Rd8 13.Rxe5 Qd6 14.Qf4! and White had recouped his investment with interest. Little of this, of course, could be seen when playing 1.Nd5, but the two white bishops pointing at the enemy king, the open e-file making it so difficult for Black to bring his pieces over to defend, and White's chance to open further lines for his rooks by advancing the h-pawn all added up to the ingredients for a successful attack.

24 hierarchies of thought

We have already (in Sections 1, 2 and 13) touched on the distinctions between precise calculation and fuzzy thought, and the interplay between strategy and tactics. But there is another level of thought that is the key to understanding good chess.

The best way to explain it is by considering our thoughts to be arranged in a hierarchical structure. At level zero, we have precise calculation. Has the opponent's last move left him open to a killer punch? If not, does it threaten anything that demands immediate action? At level two, we browse the static features of the position – the pawn formations, the weak squares, the safety of the kings, the potential endgame advantages and other such elements that lead to the formation of a general strategy. But the real hard work goes on at the intermediate level one, where tactics and strategy play equal roles. Here's roughly how it works.

You start at level zero, sorting out the immediate tactics of the position. If that reveals no clearly best move, you move up to level two, where some fuzzy thought suggest moves that may help with strategic objectives. Those moves are sent to level zero for a tactical health check and any passed fit move to level one to be looked at in more detail. For it is here that we assess the strategic gains that may be made by tactical means. And when those are established, they must be referred back to level two, because such discoveries may lead to a modification of our entire strategy.

This constant interplay between strategy and tactics is an essential, if sometimes confusing, part of good thinking. Like a novelist's two modes of creating (when ideas are left to flow) and editing (when precise words and expressions are chosen), vague strategic planning (creative) and precise tactics (editing) require different levels of concentration. Here's a practical tip:

> **Think strategies when it's your opponent's turn to move; sort out the tactics while your own clock is running.**

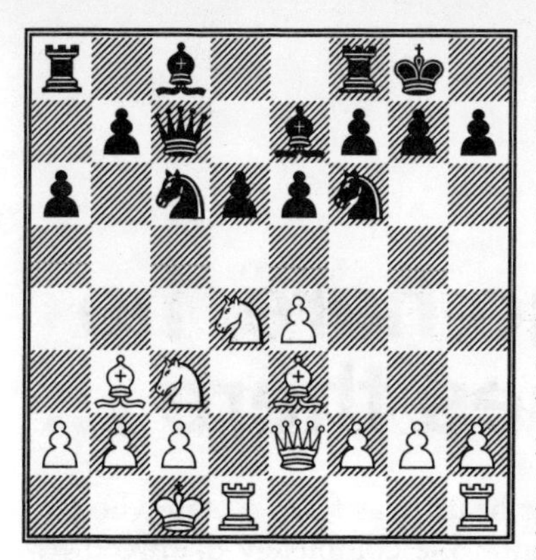

White to play. Our strategic judgement suggests 1.g4, but how do the tactics work out?

Here's an example of the hierarchical thought process.

Level 0 1...Nxe4 isn't a threat, because the pawn is defended; 1...Nxd4 is no worry, because it only brings my bishop or rook to d4. 1.Nxc6 bxc6 is good for Black, because it strengthens his centre and opens the b-file.

Level 2 With the kings castled on opposite wings, I should advance my K-side pawns to breach his defences and open lines for my rooks. The obvious plan is g4, g5, h4, h5 and g6.

Level 0 1.g4 Nxd4 2.Bxd4 (or Rxd4) e5 creates a double attack on d4 (with the pawn) and g4 (with bishop and knight). I could save the g-pawn with 2.Rxd4 e5 3.Rc4, but it leaves my rook looking rather stupid on c4.

Level 1 But if Black does play Nxd4 and e5, his ...e5 loses him control of d5 and makes my bishop on b3 much more powerful. Also, when he takes the pawn on g4, it opens the g-file for my rook.

Level 2 If he is going to weaken his white squares by playing e5, it could be a considerable advantage to me to eliminate his white-squared bishop ...

Level 1 ... so I might even consider 1.g4 Nxd4 2.Rxd4 e5 3.Rc4 Qd8 4.Rxc8!? Rxc8 5.g5 with h4, h5 and g6 to follow.

Level 0 ... or I could avoid all that trouble by preparing g4 with 1.Rg1.

Level 2 So there are three possible plans: 1.g4 Nxd4 2.Bxd4 e5 3.Be3, giving up the g-pawn and relying on control of d5 and the open g-file for compensation; or 1.g4 Nxd4 2.Rxd4 e5 3.Rc4 Qd8 4.Rxc8, giving up the exchange and relying on the K-side pawn storm; or 3.Rg1, not giving up anything.

And deciding among those takes us to level three in the hierarchy, which is, at present, out of our depth.

25 I go here, he goes there ...

One of the best excuses I ever heard was from a man who had just lost to a female opponent. 'She completely disrupted my thought processes,' he complained. 'Every time I tried to calculate something, I'd begin: "I go here, he goes there," and then I'd have to correct myself: "No, it's I go here, *she* goes there".'

Quite apart from providing a ready-made excuse in such circumstances, the 'I go here, he goes there' method is a good habit to get into – for it is surprisingly easy to forget that little rule about White and Black making alternate moves. There are two circumstances where such a fault often occurs.

1 When both sides have clear plans that appear to have no point of interaction, trying to analyse them properly can seem like trying to sing two different songs at the same time, alternating the notes of one with those of the other.
2 When you have followed a forcing variation for several moves, but can't quite see what your opponent's next move is likely to be.

> Sometimes, when you can't find a move for your opponent, it's because he hasn't got one.

It is surprisingly easy to reject a very strong move because you cannot see how your opponent defends against it. When your opponent has only one defence to your threats, you will certainly continue your analysis, but when he has no defence at all, there is the temptation to reject the whole line and look at something different simply because you cannot see how to continue the analysis. 'I go here, he goes nowhere at all' may be the real signpost to victory.

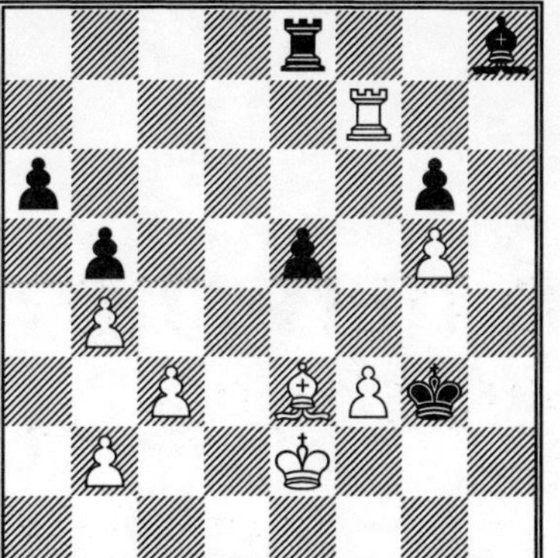

From Fischer–Reshevsky, US Championship 1962–3. White to play; he's a pawn up and has the position under firm control. The great Bobby Fischer played 1.Kd3, correctly analysing that 1...Rd8+ 2.Ke4 Rd1 fails to give Black the desired counterplay because 3.Rh7 will only force the rook back to d8 to defend the bishop.

What was the stronger move that Fischer overlooked? Indeed, it is so strong that it leaves almost nothing to analyse at all.

The answer is 1.Kf1! taking the g2-square away from Black's king, and thereby threatening 2.Bf2+ Kh3 3.Rh7 mate, a threat so strong that White's mind wandered off to look at something else instead. Since 1...Kh4 2.Kg2 or 1...Kh3 2.Bf2 closes the net, again threatening 3.Rh7 mate in either case, Black has nothing better than to jettison his bishop with 1...Bg7 to stave off the mate threat.

To some extent 1.Kf1 is an unnatural move to consider, since it is a retreating move when the centralizing Kd3 and Ke4 is beckoning. Yet with Black's king so short of squares, it should be quite natural to look at the move that cuts its options down further. The trouble is, it is simply too strong. Black has no reply at all, so there is nothing to analyse.

I play 1.Kf1, he goes nowhere. End of game.

part two
advanced

The philosopher Ludwig Wittgenstein likened the process of increasing one's conceptual understanding of a topic to that of climbing a ladder to a higher plane. The ladder serves to lift you from one level to another, but once you have succeeded in climbing it, you may kick it away, because you will never need it again. Any rule of thumb may be a rung on such a ladder. The rook on the seventh rank, pawns on the opposite colour square to one's bishop, weak squares, bad bishops and most of the other handy clichés we embrace to save us from positional howlers are all specific examples of far more general rules of piece co-ordination that one can learn only through experience.

When a poor player asks a stronger one why one move is better than another in a particular position, and no convincing tactical reason is available, the stronger player may select a handful of appropriate slogans from his collection that appear to justify it, but it is very unlikely that such rules formed part of his reasoning in selecting the move in the first place. He didn't put his pawn on a black square because he had a white-squared bishop; he played the pawn move because it felt the right thing to do. That particular ladder, of rules relating to pawns and bishops, has been kicked away and replaced by a higher level of understanding.

Try these two typical conversations between Mr Black (a good player) and Mr White (a better one).

Conversation One

B When you needed to give your king an escape square, why did you play h3 instead of g3?

W With a black-squared bishop, it's more logical to play h3. If I'd played g3, my entire position would have been riddled with white-square weaknesses.

B I understand now. Thank you for explaining it.

Conversation Two

B When you needed to give your king an escape square, why did you play g3 instead of h3?

W With the endgame approaching, I want my king nearer the centre, so g3 is more logical to let the king move to g2 rather than h2. Anyway, with a black-squared bishop, it's better to play g3 to strengthen the black squares still further. The king can look after the white ones from g2.

B Now I understand. Thank you for explaining it.

The funny thing is that both players are quite likely to be taken in by what they said on each occasion. The principles of positional chess are by no means as absolute as we are led to believe.

The great Latvian world champion Mikhail Tal once told of his bemusement when his opponent in a world title match, Mikhail Botvinnik, after very little thought exchanged a pair of rooks on an open file, then moved his second rook away from the same file. After the game Tal confessed his surprise at the decision. 'This type of position,' Botvinnik explained to him, 'one must play not with two pairs of rooks, nor with no rooks at all, but only with one pair of rooks.' Tal went home and spent many hours analysing the various endgames with two rooks, one rook and no rooks each, finally concluding that Botvinnik's position could be saved only in the case of the single rook. His analyses, in fact, taught him so much about such endgames that he was able, with confidence, to say from that moment on that 'such positions' should be played with just one rook. Neither Botvinnik nor Tal, however, would have been able to explain precisely what they meant by 'such positions'.

In this second section of the book, we shall re-examine some of the principles enunciated in the earlier pages and try to move towards an understanding of the meta-principles behind them. You may, like Mikhail Tal, find it heavy going and confusing at first, but confusion is often an essential part of the learning process, especially in chess where most players find, as they progress, that the game alternates between phases of seeming quite easy, then impossibly difficult.

The ideas I have tried to explain in the earlier pages are the ones most players stick at for the majority of their chess lives. Some players are even quite happy to continue making the same meta-errors for most of their careers. They just reach a plateau of understanding that lets them play decent enough chess, without really trying to move to a higher level. The sections that follow are the next 25 ladders to be climbed and kicked away.

26 the good 'bad bishop'

Like church dignitaries, from an archbishop down to the humblest deacon, there is a notional pecking order of bishops on the chessboard. At the highest level, we have the good, indeed almost saintly bishop, with unimpeded access to squares of one colour, and its pawns standing on the opposite colour, letting its influence be felt in all four corners of the board simultaneously.

Next, you might have thought, should come the not-quite-so-good bishop, largely unimpeded but with local difficulties in one small area. But you would be wrong. For only just behind the extremely good bishop comes the good 'bad bishop'.

> A good 'bad bishop' is better than a bad 'good bishop'.

Think back to why a 'bad bishop' is bad. It is bad because of the weaknesses on the squares it does not control. Looking at that more optimistically, however, just think of the squares it does control. With pawns and bishop controlling the same colour squares, they may bring unrivalled power to bear over half the board. When a 'bad bishop' is not blocked in behind its own pawns, it can be a formidable attacking piece.

So continuing with our classification of clergy, we follow the saintly bishop with the good 'bad bishop' – the bishop that is existentially bad, but for that very reason becomes a powerful attacking piece. Then comes the mostly good bishop – serving a positive bad bishop's defensive function on one wing, while able to attack (in the style of a good bishop) on the other. Only just behind him comes the not-so-bad bishop, which performs the important function of defending a weak pawn (we'll meet a good example of him in Section 67). And finally the utterly bad bishop, who can only look on blindly while his position is being invaded on squares of the opposite colour.

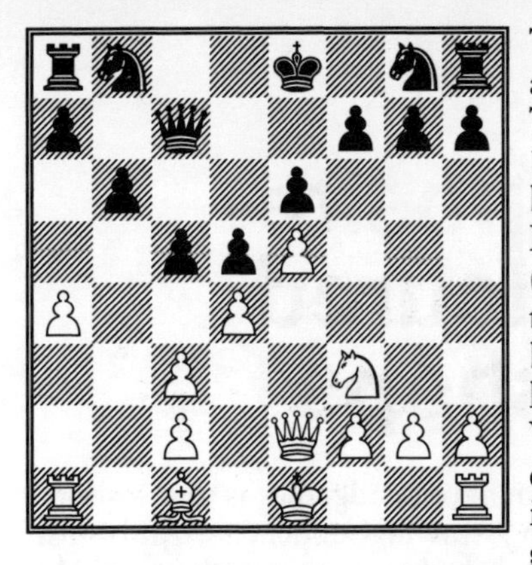

This position was reached after ten moves of the game Tal–Donner, Wijk aan Zee 1968. After the central pawns became locked together, Black exchanged his good (black-squared) bishop for the knight on c3, then played b6 and Ba6 to rid himself of his bad bishop. Now, if White does not play actively enough, he can easily drift into a bad bishop versus good knight endgame, with the additional problem of doubled c-pawns and Black having the chance of invading with his rooks down the c-file. Now watch how Tal handled the white pieces.

1.a5! bxa5 2.Ba3! Nd7 3.dxc5 Ne7 4.c6!

Everything is done to enhance the effect of the bishop: a5 removed a defender from c5 to make the a3–f8 diagonal more difficult to keep closed; 4.c6 jettisoned a pawn to open the diagonal.

4...Qxc6 5.0-0 Qxc3

Not so much greed as the need to prevent Nd4, Nb5 and Nd6+.

6.Rfd1 Nc6 7.Bd6 Qc4 8.Qe3 Qe4 9.Qb3 Nb6 10.c4! Qxc4

10...Nxc4 would have lost immediately to 11.Qb7

11.Qa3 Qa6 12.Rac1 Rc8 13.Nd2! f6

Otherwise 14.Qg3 is hard to meet – thanks to the influence of the bad bishop on d6.

14.exf6 gxf6 15.Qf3 Kd7 16.Qxf6! Rhe8

16...Kxd6 would have led to mate after 17.Ne4+ Kc7 18.Nc5! Qe2 19.Qg7+ Kd6 20.Nb7 mate.

17.Ne4 Ne7 18.Nc5+ Rxc5 19.Bxc5 Nc4 20.Bxe7

The bad bishop has the last word. After 20...Rxe7, 21.Rxd5+! is decisive.

Black resigned.

2 opposite-coloured bishops

One of the first things we learn about endgames is that bishops of opposite colour have strong drawing tendencies. And most players spend the rest of their lives believing it to be true. Yet half the time, the exact opposite is the case.

What is certainly true is that in endgames in which each side has only one bishop and a handful of pawns left, and the bishops travel on opposite-coloured squares, an advantage of one pawn is, more often than not, insufficient to win. Even a two-pawn advantage often leads only to a draw. If the defender can blockade the extra pawns on squares their bishop cannot control, all attempts to advance them may come to a complete halt.

Yet when other pieces, particularly rooks, also remain on the board, the presence of bishops of opposite colour tend to increase the winning prospects of the side with the initiative. The reason is simple: if your bishop can find something to attack, it can tie a larger piece down to a passive defensive role, since anything one bishop can attack, the other cannot defend.

Once such a concession has been forced, the way is clear to advance a passed pawn, if you have one, or improve the position of your king, or initiate a general pawn advance to stifle your opponent further. As long as you can prevent your opponent from finding a way to liquidate, even at the cost of a pawn, into a pure bishop endgame, such positions can offer good winning chances.

In the middlegame, all of the above is even more valid. When opposite-coloured bishops are on the board, it can even seem as though the attacker is playing with an extra piece. A black-squared bishop is not much use in defending against a white-squared attack.

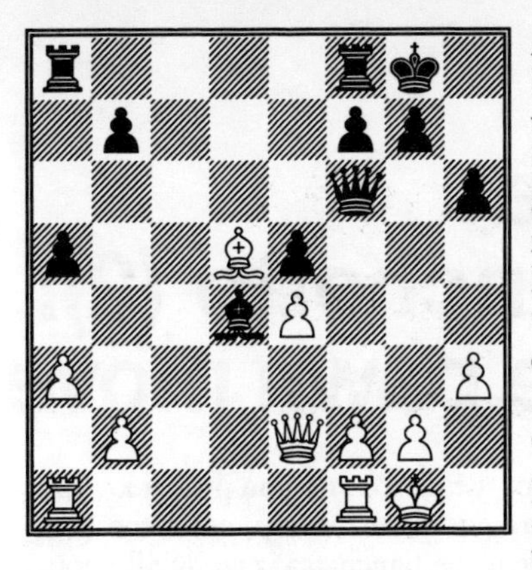

A classic opposite-coloured bishops game from the 1929 world championship match between Bogolyubov (White) and Alekhine. It is White's move and since 1.Bxb7 lets Black regain the pawn with 1...Rb8, the most natural continuation seems to be 1.Rac1 Rac8, some friendly exchanges on the c-file, and a quick draw. Now watch how Bogolyubov squeezed something out of the position.

1.Rad1! Rac8 2.Rd3! Rc7 3.b3 b5 4.Rf3 Qb6 5.a4 bxa4 6.bxa4 Qb4 7.Qa2 Qb2 8.Qxb2 Bxb2 9.Rb1 Bd4 10.Rb5 Ra7 11.h4 h5 12.Rb7! Rxb7 13.Bxb7 Rd8 14.Bd5 Rd7

The rook has escaped from f8, but it is still doomed to passivity.

15.Rb3 Kf8 16.Rb5 Ra7 17.Bb7 Ke7 18.g3 Kd6 19.Kg2 Kc7 20.Bd5 Kd6 21.f4 f6 22.Bb3!

Preparing to slide back with Bd1 and win the h-pawn (since g6 may always be met by f5).

22...Ra6 23.Bf7 Rc6 24.Rd5+ Ke7 25.Bxh5 Rc5 26.fxe5 fxe5 27.Bf3! Kf6

After 27...Rxd5 28.exd5, Black's e-pawn is irrelevant and White is effectively two pawns ahead.

28.Rd6+ Ke7 29.Rg6 Kf8 30.Bh5! Be3 31.Kf3 Rc3 32.Ke2 Bc5 33.Re6! g6

A desperate remedy against the threat of Re8 mate, but now the game is effectively over. The remaining moves were 34.Bxg6 Re3+ 35.Kd1 Rxg3 36.h5 Kg7 (the main threat was 37.h6 and 38.Re8 mate) 37.Rxe5 Bb4 38.Ke2 Ra3 39.Be8 Rh3 40.Bd7 Rc3 41.Re6 Bf8 42.Ra6 Bb4 43.h6+ Kf7 44.Be6+ Kf6 45.Bf5+ Kf7 46.Ra7+ Be7 47.Rxa5 Rc2+ 48.Kd3 Rb2 49.h7 Bf6 50.e5 Bg7 51.Ra7+ Kf8 52.e6 Be5 53.e7+ resigns.

Black's 11...h5 (played to prevent White's threat of h5) and his 21...f6 may be open to criticism, but the whole endgame is a fine example of the pressure that can be created with bishops of opposite colours.

28 the fianchetto (2): the pawn move

We met, in Section 12, the idea of the *fianchetto*: you push a knight's pawn one square forwards to get your bishop onto the long diagonal. Now we'll tell you what the fianchetto is really all about. Don't think about the bishop move; think about the pawn move.

In any strategy, the pawns come first. They define each player's territory and determine the middlegame plans. Sometimes, admittedly, the main objective of a fianchetto is to get the bishop on the long diagonal, but just as often, the pawn move is what really matters. Nowhere is this more clear than in the King's Indian Defence.

When Mikhail Chigorin first experimented with the idea of playing for ...e5 against White's 1.d4, his system began with 1.d4 Nf6 2.c4 d6 3.Nf3 Nbd7 4.Nc3 e5 5.e4 Be7. Then it might continue 6.Be2 0-0 7.0-0 Re8 8.d5 Bf8, after which Black's natural plan is to prepare f5 by playing g6, Bg7, perhaps even Rf8 and retreating the knight from f6.

Out of that system grew the King's Indian Defence: 1.d4 Nf6 2.c4 g6 3.Nc3 Bg7 4.e4 d6. Black's idea is to play for e5, when White's d5 may be met by Ne8 (or Nfd7 or Nh5) and f5, with the g-pawn ready to recapture on f5 after exf5. The whole thing makes sense because if White does play d5, then the g-pawn is in the right place to support f5, while if the d-pawn stays on d4, Black has the option of playing exd4, leaving the bishop on g7 with a nice open diagonal.

It looks highly suspicious playing 2...g6 in the expectation that a later ...e5 will be met by d5, when the need to fight for space will demand a pawn on g6 to support the f5 advance – it all seems like putting up the decorations before the walls have been plastered, but modern refined opening systems are full of such clever ideas.

Looked at the other way round, it seems curious to put a bishop on g7, then block its diagonal with e5. But e5 was the main idea all along, the pawn went to g6 to be ready with f5 when the e-pawn needed a neighbour to join it on the fourth rank, and the bishop went to g7 to plug the black-squared holes.

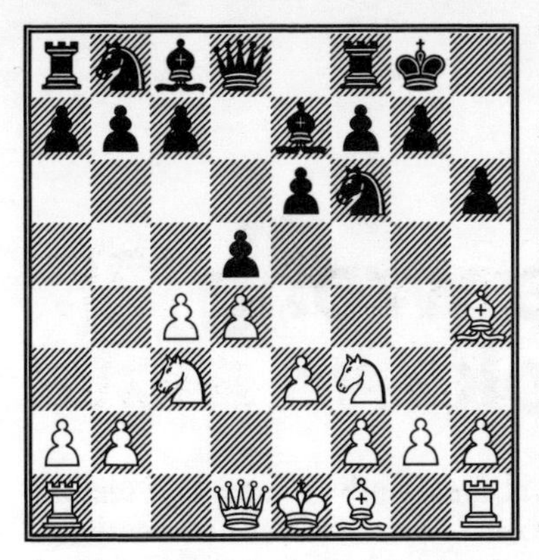

This position in the Queen's Gambit Declined is reached after the moves 1.d4 d5 2.c4 e6 3.Nc3 Nf6 4.Bg5 Be7 5.e3 h6 6.Bh4 0-0 7.Nf3 when one of Black's most popular responses is 7...b6.

Well obviously, with his pawn on e6, Black is playing the move in order to give his white-squared bishop something to look forward to. With its natural line of development blocked, it looks forward to a new life on the long diagonal.

But that's only half the story. Look at the central pawns. What happens if White exchanges pawns on d5? If cxd5 is met by exd5, Black will want to advance c5 and recapture with a pawn after dxc5 to keep his centre pawns together. So the pawn on b6 has another important function besides just letting the bishop develop.

The most common continuation after 7...b6 used to be 8.cxd5 Nxd5 9.Bxe7 Qxe7 10.Nxd5 exd5 11.Rc1 when, for many years, Black players would automatically continue 11...Bb7. Once you have played b6, it is only good sense to put the bishop on b7. That's what the move was for. As soon as somebody had the original idea of playing 11...Be6 instead, however, everyone realized that it was obviously much better. Next move, or the move after, Black will play c5 and hope to gain counterplay later by advancing his Q-side pawns further. The bishop is far better placed on e6 to counter any White plans for a K-side attack than it would be if it were buried on b7.

In this case, 7...b6 is a pawn move in its own right, not just half a bishop move.

26 the wrong rook

A well-trained rook will froth at the mouth as soon as it sees an open file and fly directly onto it – correct? Well, not entirely. When an open file offers the rook a chance to advance and attack enemy weaknesses, or when conceding the file to the opponent's rooks would let him do the same thing, it may be the best place to be, but sometimes a rook does better lurking on a not-yet-open file, in preparation for a predictable opening of the position.

Remember too that a pawn with a rook behind it is one of the happiest combinations of pieces. The rook supports the pawn's advance, and the advancing pawn creates more space for the rook.

> Rooks are the most efficient power behind advancing pawns.

When you have decided which file needs a rook, there is still the question of which rook. More often than not, you must take a decision before you know what future demands will be placed on your rook. If the c-file offers good prospects for one white rook, do you play Rac1, leaving the other rook free for later action in the centre, or Rfc1, enabling its colleague to join in the Q-side action from a1 or b1?

Whichever you choose, it is likely to turn out to be the wrong rook. A small part of the art of good strategy is to keep one's options open until the opponent has committed his rooks. Then take the decisions that leave his rooks tripping over each other's feet.

The late Dutch grandmaster Jan Hein Donner once pointed out how effective it can be – both strategically and psychologically – to respond immediately to a long-deliberated rook move with a reply that makes it seem ill-judged. If White chooses Rac1, then Black opens the a- or b-file; if he plays Rfc1, he opens the e- or d-file. And the longer White thought about his rook move, the greater the impact of proving to him that it was the wrong rook.

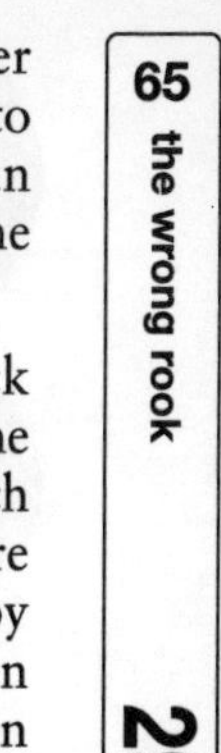

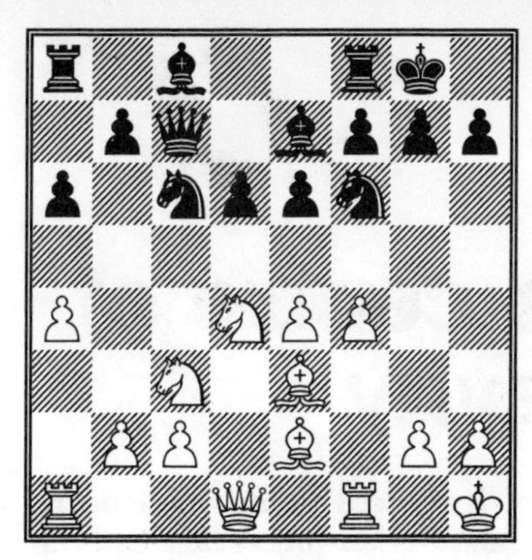

A standard position (after eleven moves with Black to play) from the Sicilian Defence. Where should he place his rooks?

In the near future, Black would like to expand on the Q-side by playing b5, which makes b8 an attractive square for a rook, but if b5 is met by an exchange of pawns, then the a-file will become open and a rook may be useful on a8. The c-file is half-open, which makes c8 an obvious candidate too, while d8 looks useful, to be ready for an opening of the d-file after either e5 or ...d5, and e8 is also attractive in case of f5 or ...e5. Finally, there's a case to be made for leaving a rook on f8, so that White's attacking plan of advancing g4 and g5 may be met by an eventual ...f6. Now look how Garry Kasparov handled his rooks from this position in the final, world-title winning game against Karpov in 1985.

11...Re8 (ready for central action when necessary) **12.Bf3 Rb8** (off the bishop's diagonal and supporting a later advance of the b-pawn) **13.Qd2 Bd7 14.Nb3 b6 15.g4 Bc8 16.g5 Nd7 17.Qf2 Bf8 18.Bg2 Bb7 19.Rad1 g6 20.Bc1 Rbc8** (on to the half-open file – but not for long) **21.Rd3 Nb4 22.Rh3 Bg7 23.Be3 Re7! 24.Kg1 Rce8!!**

Since Qh4 can always be met by Nf8, White's attack can only make progress by playing f5. (24.Kg1 was also preparation for this move, getting his king off the long white diagonal which will be opened if f5 is met by exf5.) Black therefore doubles rooks on the closed file to ensure that they will rage into action if White dares play f5. Let's see how the game continued.

25.Rd1 f5! 26.gxf6 (26.exf5 exf5 again leaves the black rooks looking beautiful) **26...Nxf6 27.Rg3 Rf7!** (on a half-open file at last!) **28.Bxb6 Qb8 29.Be3 Nh5 30.Rg4 Nf6** and now instead of giving away his title by conceding a draw after 31.Rg3 Nh5, Karpov went down in flames after **31.Rh4? g5! 32.fxg5 Ng4 33.Qd2 Nxe3 34.Qxe3 Nxc2 35.Qb6 Ba8 36.Rxd6?** (36.Qxb8 Rxb8 is better for Black but not as bad as this) **36...Rb7!** And Black won a piece, the game, and the world championship.

30 the centre of gravity

The importance of 'the centre' is stressed in every beginner's manual, yet the centre of the board takes precedence early in the game only because we don't yet know where our pieces will be needed. Control of the centre may be needed to maintain communications between the two wings, but as the game develops, local battlefields develop elsewhere on the board, each demanding the attention of various pieces, in attack or defence.

When the central pawns have become locked together, the centre itself may become of relatively minor importance. Even when the centre is open, it may still have little effect on the real battle. Like Clapham Junction or Crewe stations on the British rail network, the centre can be a useful place to change from one destination to another, but a rather dull location at which to spend much time.

When the important action is concentrated in various different locations – perhaps around the two kings as the players attack on opposite wings, or at the various positional weaknesses that both players are trying to exploit – communication becomes all-important. When the time is not yet ripe to launch a final attack, everything is in a state of dynamic equilibrium, with the weights of various different centres of action all combining to give the position an ever-changing centre of gravity.

> A body will topple if its centre of gravity is supported only by thin air.

In the previous section, we saw Karpov's position disintegrate as his K-side attacking pieces lost touch with their colleagues on the other wing. Communications fell apart as his men drifted right and left, but lost touch with the true centre of gravity of the game, somewhere in the middle of the board.

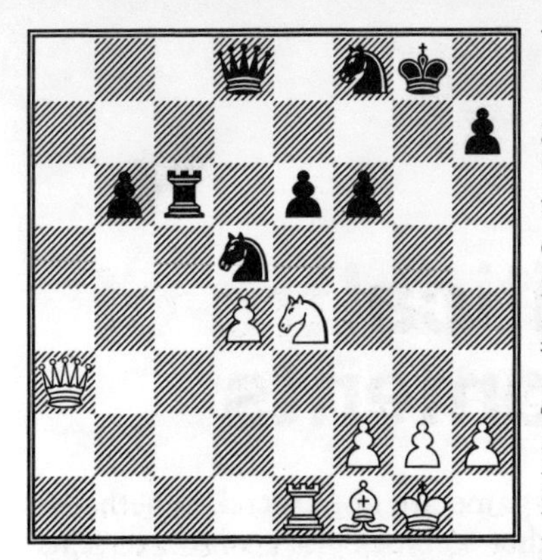

White to play (from Capablanca–Lasker, 11th game, 1921 World Championship). Black threatens to move the game's centre of gravity. What are the important features of the position and how should White react?

The position is packed with little centres of activity: the isolated pawn on d4, potentially vulnerable; the relatively exposed black king; the black pawns at e6 and f6, both needing protection; the passed pawn on b6 needing to be kept under restraint. If it were Black's move, he would play 1...f5! chasing the knight from e4. He could then continue with Rc3, cutting the white queen from the K-side, and Qf6, attacking d4. All these moves improve Black's co-ordination.

Capablanca continued with the surprising **1.h4!** The point is that 1...f5 can now be met by 2.Qg3+ Kh8 (2...Ng6 is met by 3.h5) 3.Qe5+ Kg8 4.Bb5 Rc7 5.Ng5! with a strong attack. Note how the pawn on h4 serves the double function of controlling g5 and threatening to advance to h5.

The game continued **1...Rc7 2.Qb3 Rg7 3.g3 Ra7 4.Bc4 Ra5 5.Nc3 Nxc3 6.Qxc3 Kf7 7.Qe3!** (A perfect centralizing move – combining designs on b6, e6 and h6) **7...Qd6 8.Qe4** (now eyeing b7 and h7) **8...Ra4?** (A miscalculation, but the move ought to feel wrong. The rook influences only the Q-side here. It had to retreat to a7 to stay in touch with defensive operations on the other wing.) **9.Qb7+ Kg6** (9...Kg8 10.Qc8 is just as bad). **10.Qc8 Qb4 11.Rc1 Qe7 12.Bd3+ Kh6 13.Rc7 Ra1+ 14.Kg2 Qd6 15.Qxf8+! resigns.** The white h-pawn has the last laugh: 15...Qxf8 16.Rxh7 is checkmate.

3 critical moments

Most decisions you take in a game are not crucial. Whether to exchange pieces or not, whether to block the position or leave it fluid, whether to improve the position of a bishop or a knight. Such decisions may lead to small advantages and disadvantages, which may make your task later in the game easier or more onerous. Just a few times in every game, however – it may be only once, or it may be four or five times – it really matters what you play.

> The ability to spot such critical moments is what separates genuinely strong players from mere imitations.

The ability to recognize a crisis is something that only comes with experience, but there are several warning signs to watch out for. Perhaps the most common is when a player who has had the initiative for some time begins to lose it. We saw a good example of this in the previous diagram. White, with his safer king and good bishop, has been manoeuvring against Black's weaknesses for most of the game, but natural moves fail to maintain the advantage. The move played would almost certainly not have been the first one to occur to Capablanca. It is when the natural moves fail to achieve their expected aims that you may suspect that a critical moment has been reached.

This, above all, is why a long think by a strong player is usually followed by a very precise move, while a long think by a weak player is followed by an error.

> Strong players stop to think when a crisis arrives; weak players think when they don't know what to do.

And there is a world of difference between knowing (in general terms) what to do but having to work out how to do it, and not knowing what to do in the first place.

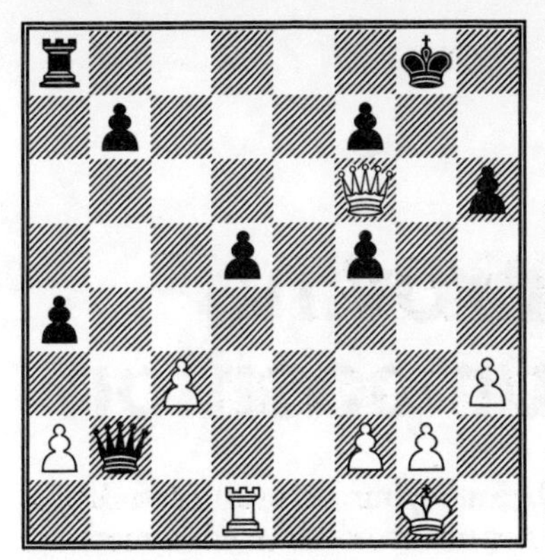

White to play, in Karpov–Vaganyan, Skopje 1976. White has succeeded in disrupting the pawn shelter around his opponent's king, but the critical moment has arrived as Black has obvious counterplay with Qxa2 and pushing his a-pawn. Precise calculation is now needed.

It would be nice to bring the rook to g3 quickly, but 1.Rd3? just loses to 1...Qb1+. The two most obvious moves are grabbing pawns with 1.Rxd5 or 1.Qxh6. The first only encourages Black's 1...Qxa2, but there is a strong temptation to play 1.Qxh6, further increasing the pressure against the black king, and think again after 1...Qxa2. Perhaps 2.Rd4 followed by Rh4 will be the way to do it.

Such sloppy thinking, however, would miss the critical nature of the position. White must think not only of Black's counterplay with Qxa2, but his possible methods of defending his king. After 1.Qxh6, Black plays 1...Ra6! followed by bringing the rook to g6. The king is then sheltered and White's attack has no way through. Now see how the game went.

1.Re1!! (stopping Ra6 because of the check on e8) **1...Qxa2 2.Qxh6 a3 3.Qg5+ Kf8 4.Qf6! Kg8** (to prevent Qh8 mate) **5.Qxf5 Qd2** (wilting under the strain; 5...d4 was the best chance to put up a fight) **6.Re7! Rf8 7.Qg4+ Kh7 8.Re5 Qh6 9.Rh5.** The queen is won and the rest is not difficult: 9...Ra8 10.Qf5+ Kg7 11.Rxh6 Kxh6 12.Qf6+ Kh7 13.Qxf7+ Kh8 14.Qxb7 resigns.

Finally, to appreciate White's play fully, we should ask why, after 1.Re1! Qxa2, Karpov did not play 2.Re3. The answer shows a surprising resource for Black: 2...f4 3.Qxf4 Qb1+ 4.Kh2 a3! 5.Rg3+ Qg6 6.Rxg6+ fxg6 and the powerful passed a-pawn ensures that White has no more than a draw.

32 improving your position

The first thing to sort out when it's your turn to move is the immediate tactics. Has your opponent overlooked something and left himself open to a damaging piece of violence? What, in turn, is he threatening that demands instant action? When you've sorted out the tactics, you remind yourself of your general strategy: what you were planning last move and what's the most useful way to move closer to the fulfilment of that plan. But what if you have no clearly formulated plan – for example when the position is too fluid for things to have settled down to enable a precise plan to be formulated? What do you do then?

A good policy is frequently to look at all your pieces and ask yourself what useful functions each is performing. Then improve the effectiveness of your most dysfunctional piece.

> Ask not what your pieces can do for you,
> ask what you can do for your pieces.

Such a policy can even lead you to find the right overall plan. Finding a useful function for one piece may easily lead to a better understanding of what the other men should be doing as well.

And when you can't quite decide which piece is not pulling its weight, there's another rather dubious maxim that may nevertheless help towards a better understanding of the position. It goes like this: when you don't know what to do, move a piece that you haven't moved for a long time. Sometimes a piece stays on the same square for so long that you think of it as a fixture. Yet it may have long outlived its original purpose on that square.

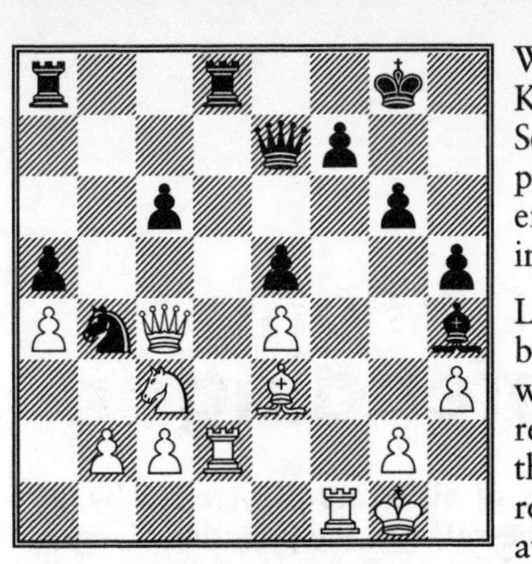

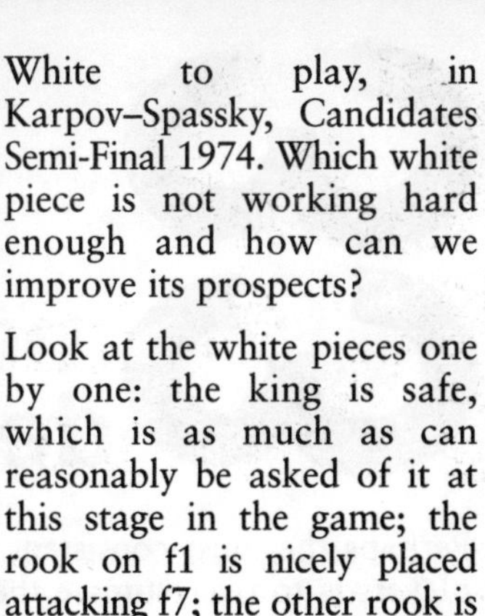

White to play, in Karpov–Spassky, Candidates Semi-Final 1974. Which white piece is not working hard enough and how can we improve its prospects?

Look at the white pieces one by one: the king is safe, which is as much as can reasonably be asked of it at this stage in the game; the rook on f1 is nicely placed attacking f7; the other rook is happy enough on the open file; the queen is beautifully situated, tying pieces to the defence of c6 and f7; the bishop on e3 is perfectly poised to attack the K-side from h6 or the Q-side from c5 or b6.

But what about the knight on c3? It looks fine, but it's not really doing much. The black c-pawn stifles any hope it might have of advancing to b5 or d5, while its only other function is to defend the pawns on a4 and e4, neither of which is remotely in need of protection.

Karpov played the excellent move **1.Nb1!!** both setting the knight on course to join the K-side attack via d2 and f3, and freeing the c3 square for a pawn. The immediate threat is 2.c3 forcing the knight away from its defence of c6.

There followed **1...Qb7** (defending c6) **2.Kh2!** (threatening to cause the bishop fatal embarrassment with 3.g3) **2...Kg7 3.c3 Na6 4.Re2!** (freeing d2 for the knight while saving the white rook for later action) **4...Rf8 5.Nd2 Bd8 6.Nf3 f6 7.Rd2! Be7 8.Qe6 Rad8 9.Rxd8 Bxd8 10.Rd1 Nb8 11.Bc5 Rh8 12.Rxd8! resigns.** (12...Rxd8 loses to 13.Be7 Re8 14.Qxf6+ Kh7 15.Qf7+ and mate next move.)

Note how it was the knight's manoeuvre to f3 that induced the weakening ...f6 which let the white queen invade on e6. Finally, it is worth pointing out that White's knight on c3 in the diagram position had been sitting there since 18 moves earlier, patiently waiting to be given something useful to do.

33 defending

Perhaps the most consistent of all errors perpetrated by club players is to overestimate the value of the initiative. Everyone likes to attack and to feel the joy of dictating the course of events, yet it is, in practice, just as easy to win games by good defence as by attacking well. A slightly passive or cramped position need not be disadvantageous in itself. As long as it contains no structural weaknesses, your position should be defensible – and when the attacking forces eventually have to retreat, it is highly probable that the attacker will, in his haste to advance, have created his own weaknesses.

The art of good defence is patience.

The attacker feels he is doing well because he limits his opponent's choice of move, yet by doing so, he may also limit his opponent's chance of making a mistake. A series of direct threats may help to wear down the opponent's resistance, but defending accurately against such threats may also cause the attacker to lose faith. Like a good baseline player in tennis, the good defender on a chessboard may, after a long period under pressure, finally catch his opponent with a good passing shot.

The point of greatest psychological vulnerability for both players is when the initial wave of an attack has been beaten back. The poor defender will then breathe a sigh of relief and make a fatal mistake instantly; the poor attacker will continue playing aggressively and leave himself open to a decisive counter-attack.

For many players, the most difficult aspect of the game is maintaining emotional equilibrium as the position changes from good to bad. Keeping calm under pressure is the essence of good defensive play.

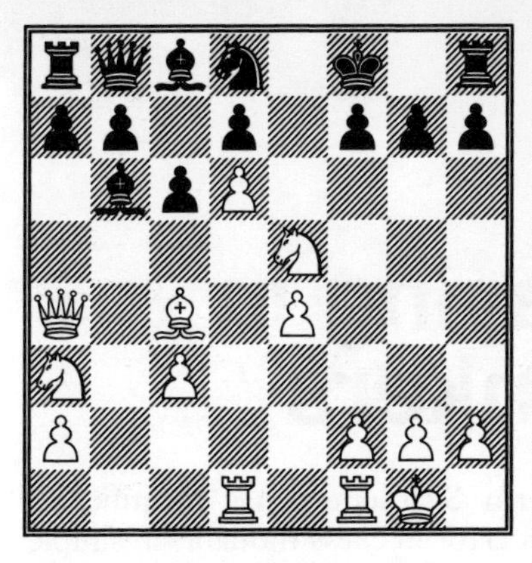

The first official world champion, Wilhelm Steinitz, made a practice of defending the most awful-looking positions. He must have known that some of the positions he willingly adopted were objectively almost as bad as they looked, but he also understood the curious tensions that may be created in the mind of the player on the other side of the board.

The diagram position was reached after Mikhail Chigorin's 15th move as White against Steinitz in the 15th game of their world title match in 1889. With his entire Q-side locked out of the game, Black's position looks – and objectively is – a disaster. Yet Steinitz willingly entered such a position many times. The continuation of this game shows why: **15...f6 16.Nf3 Bc5 17.e5!** (a correct sacrifice of a piece) **17...b5 18.Bxb5 cxb5 19.Nxb5 Ne6!** (keeping the white knight out of c7 and queen away from f4) **20.exf6 gxf6 21.Qh4 Kf7** (21...Qxb5 would have lost to 22.Qxf6+ Kg8 23.Ne5 with a devastating attack) **22.Qh5+ Kg8? 23.Qg4+? Kf7 24.Qh5+ Kg7!**

By now, both players had noticed that White should have met 22...Kg8 with 23.Qe8+ Kg7 24.Qe7+ Kg8 25.Ne5! fxe5 26.Rd3 with a winning attack. Now, after 24...Kg7, what is White to do? He can draw with 25.Qg4+, but that would be letting Black get away with his terrible play earlier in the game. Chigorin decided to continue the attack with **25.Nfd4**, but after **25...Bxd4 26.Nxd4 Rf8! 27.Rd3 Bb7 28.Nxe6+ dxe6 29.Rh3 Be4 30.Qg4+ Bg6** his pawns were no match for Black's extra piece. The game concluded 31.Qxe6 Qb6 32.Qd5 Rad8 33.Rd1 Rfe8 34.c4 Rxd6! 35.Qf3 Rd3! 36.Qg4 Re4 White resigned.

playing in blinkers

The Finnish psychologist Pertti Saariluoma has identified a remarkably common source of error in chess thought. In simple terms, it happens when you become so fixated on one move or variation that it produces an inhibiting effect on all other thoughts. You start thinking about a tempting rook move advancing down a file, and you overlook a more powerful sideways move of the same rook; you think so long about prospects of moving your knight forwards that you never consider a powerful retreat; you are so proud of one piece powerfully established on a strong square that you miss the chance to force a simple win with a sequence beginning with its exchange for a passively placed enemy piece.

These common errors are all connected with the way we perceive chess positons. With up to 32 pieces scattered over 64 squares, and our poor brains generally incapable of juggling more than seven items at the same time, we need to codify the pieces into meaningful subsets. We don't think in terms of discrete pieces on their individual squares, but instead understand a position in terms of the relationships between groups of pieces. The trouble is that such a process is liable to lock us into particular mind-sets. When, for example, we have a queen and bishop on the same diagonal, their relationship exerts such a pull on our thoughts that it can blind us to possible moves of the queen or bishop on their other diagonals.

Good ideas interfere with better ones.

The only solution – though difficult to put into practice – is to train yourself to look again at each move of a variation in a fresh and naïve manner. Somehow, you have to put your previous thoughts aside and clear a path in your mind to let radically new ideas come through.

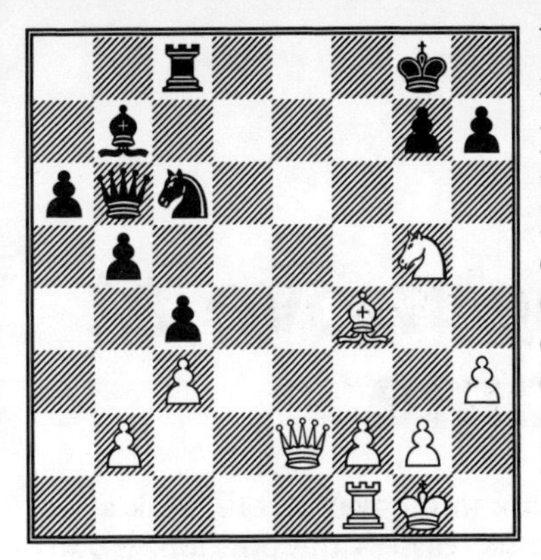

White to play. Mate in how many?

Positions such as this were used in the experiments that led Saariluoma to his conclusions about interference effects in chess thinking. The conversation between experimenter (E) and subject (S) usually went on these lines.

E White to play; how many moves does it take him to force mate?
S (after a brief thought) Five.
E Is there any way of forcing mate in fewer than five moves?
S Only if Black makes a mistake.
E But if Black plays correctly, are you sure White cannot force mate in under five moves?
S (after peering suspiciously around the board and counting on his fingers) I'm sure.
E If I told you there was a mate in four, would you believe me?
S (more suspicious peering) No.

The subject has spotted immediately good old Philidor's mate: 1.Qe6+ Kh8 2.Nf7+ Kg8 3.Nh6+ Kh8 4.Qg8+ Rxg8 5.Nf7 mate, which is such a strong piece of routine in such positions that it makes it very difficult to see 1.Qe6+ Kh8 2.Nf7+ Kg8 3.Nd8+! Kh8 (or 3...Kf8 4.Qf7 mate) 4.Qe8 mate. Once you have set the mental mechanism in motion with Qe6+ and Nf7+, it gets carried along on the current of experience, missing the short cut.

35 one move at a time

There is a considerable paradox in the way we all think about chess. Every move, we pause to reassess the position, modify our plan, and select the move that appears to fit in best with our objectives and frustrate those of our opponent. We think in terms of plans and formations and the flow of a strategic path. Yet on the other hand, we are making a set of discrete moves, each time seeking the single move that is best in this particular position, with past history having nothing to do with it. Long-term plans are merely a set of devices that steer us towards individual moves.

> History is all in the past.

The strongest players have the ability – and the considerable mental energy needed – to approach each position on its own merits irrespective of what went before. Countless opportunities are missed by players who blindly pursue last move's plan without taking account of a crucial change of circumstances.

One of the great advantages that computer chess programs have over human players is their ability to treat each position as a new problem. Humans find good moves by thinking in terms of thematic moves and positional concepts; machines look at everything and consequently stumble across unthematic, anti-positional but nonetheless powerful ideas that would be all too easy for a human to reject on principle. There can be considerable advantages in taking things one move at a time.

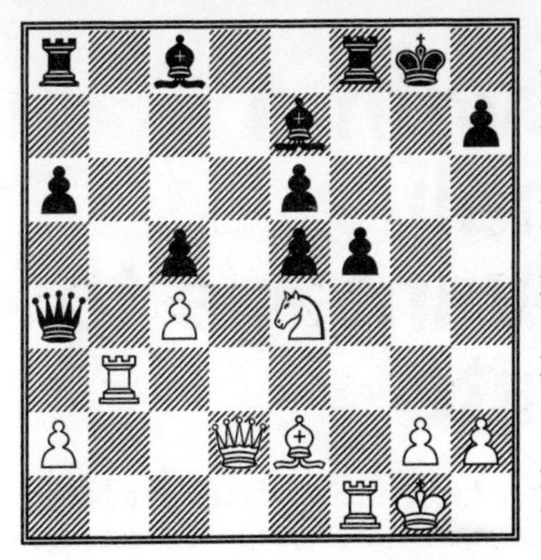

Confessions of a misspent youth, No. 1: from Hartston–Gligoric, Hastings 1964–5. White to play.

Black has just advanced his pawn from c6 to c5 in order to provide his queen with a path to retreat to e8 to aid the defence. If he had played ...fxe4 instead, he would have been quickly mated by Rg3+ followed by Rxf8+ and Qg5.

After ...c5, however, my thoughts were still a move or two behind the game. White can win immediately with **1.Rg3+ Kh8** (1...Kf7 2.Bh5 is immediate mate) **2.Qc3!** when there is not the glimmer of a defence to the threat of Qxe5+. Instead I played 1.Qh6? Rf7 2.Rg3+ Kh8, certain that h6 and g3 were where the queen and rook belonged.

Two moves before the diagram, the black f-pawn had been on f6 securely defending e5. At that stage, any idea of Qc3 would have been quite pointless, so I had mentally booked the queen a ride to h6 and was too slow to change the ticket.

The tale, however, had a happy ending: after 1.Qh6 Rf7 2.Rg3+ Kh8 there followed 3.Bh5 Qe8 (forced) 4.Rxf5!! exf5 5.Nd6! Bxd6 6.Bxf7 resigns. After 6...Qxf7 7.Qxd6, Black cannot defend all of d8, e5, f6 and f8 from the white queen and even 7...h5, to give the king an escape on h7, opens the way for 8.Qh6+ Qh7 9.Qf8+. By missing the 'obvious' win, I forced myself to find something far more elegant.

36 … with a small advantage to white

Can a position turn from 'better for White' to 'better for Black' without anyone making a mistake? That is a fundamental question of the philosophy of positional assessment and nobody, as far as I can tell, has ever even addressed it. The game of chess, though undeniably offering more possibilities than anyone can ever hope to calculate, is undeniably finite. Any position therefore must, in theory, be objectively solvable as a win for White, win for Black or draw. The phrase 'better for White' can have only a subjective meaning.

In practice, it means one of two things:

1 in my opinion, this position is a draw or a win for White, but I'm not sure which; or
2 over the next few moves, Black is going to have far more practical opportunities to go wrong than White.

There seems no convincing reason that the second of these should not turn into a 'better for Black' some moves later, without a mistake on White's part. As a simple example, one may take a position in which one side has a promising attack to compensate for a structural weakness. The defender may have to play extremely accurately for a long period just to survive, but when he emerges unscathed, the advantage has passed to his side, though still perhaps not enough to force victory.

> Stronger players think in terms of strengths and weaknesses rather than overall advantage and disadvantage.

A club player, sighting a promising attack, will think: 'White is winning.' A club champion will think: 'White has a clear advantage.' A master will think: 'Now Black must start to work a little.'

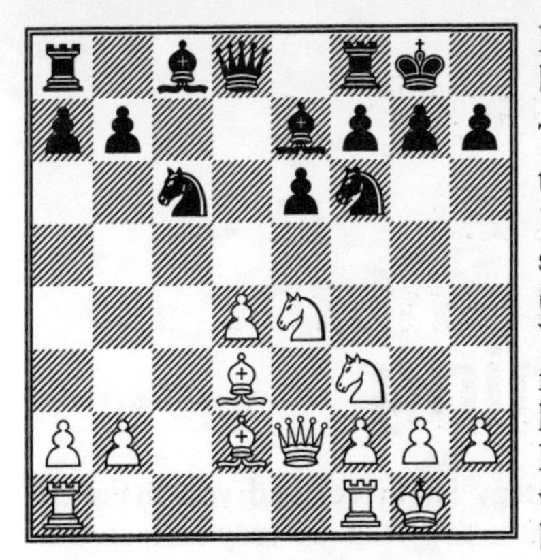

Black to play. Who stands better?

This position was reached twice in early games of the 1996 Fide World Championship between Gata Kamsky (White) and Anatoly Karpov. White's pieces are well placed for a K-side attack, but he has an isolated d-pawn. Black has no structural weaknesses, but is a little behind in development and rather cramped. He cannot risk taking the d-pawn since 1...Nxd4 2.Nxd4 Qxd4 3.Bc3 would leave all the white pieces pointing at Black's king.

In the second game of the match, Karpov continued 1...Bd7 and there followed 2.Rad1 Rc8 3.Rfe1 Nd5 4.Nc3 Nf6 5.a3 Qc7 6.Bg5! Qa5 7.d5! exd5 8.Bxf6 Bxf6 9.Bxh7+! Kxh7 10.Rxd5! leading to a clear advantage to White, since 10...Qc7 is met by 11.Qd3+ winning the bishop on d7. (Karpov in fact gave up his queen with 10...Bxc5 11.Rxa5 Bxa5, but after 12.b4! soon found himself struggling.)

When the same position was reached two games later, Karpov played 1...Qb6! There followed 2.a3 Bd7 3.Rfd1 Rad8 4.Nxf6+ Bxf6 5.Qe4 g6 6.Be3 Ne7 7.Ne5 Nf5 8.Nc4 Qa6! when objectively White has nothing better than suing for peace with 9.Ne5. Instead Kamsky continued 9.a4?! Bc6 10.Qf4 Bd5 11.Ne5 Qb6 and Black had everything he wanted: a secure king, a complete blockade of the d-pawn and even the possibility of meeting 12.g4 with 12...g5!

So who stands 'better' in the diagram position? A good attacking player will always prefer White; a solid defender with a good positional sense will prefer Black. And both will be quite correct.

timing

Even when your general strategy is correct and you make no mistakes in calculation, it is still depressingly easy to lose. For having a good strategy and implementing that strategy correctly are two very different things. At the highest level of chess though, it all comes down to a question of timing. When should you switch from cautious circumspection to all-out attack? When is it safe to move from passive defence to fighting for the initiative?

> There are two easy ways to spoil a good position: doing nothing when you should be doing something, and doing something when you should be doing nothing.

The first question you should be constantly asking yourself is: 'How can I improve my position?' The next question is: 'How can my opponent improve his position?' When you have the advantage – in time, space, material or general mobility – and all your men are effectively placed, then is the moment to launch an attack, before your opponent catches up. A correct attack stems from surplus capacity: kings need defending; important central squares need to be kept under guard; the opponent's expansionist dreams need to be held back; but if there are any pieces left over when those tasks are done, they must attack the enemy.

When the balance of power is delicately poised, however, and both sides are still disputing vital areas of the board, any attempt to launch an attack is liable to result in a loss of control once any temporary initiative has been dissipated. In tense positions, 'doing nothing' (but doing it very well) is often the best policy.

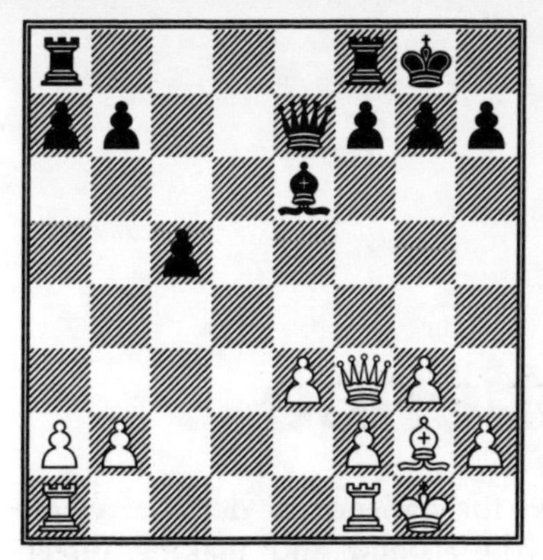

White to play, from Marshall–Capablanca, 1909. How should he plan his next few moves? Should he begin with 1.Qxb7, or 1.Rfc1, or something else entirely?

The position looks innocuous enough, but with rival pawn majorities on opposite wings, both sides should be thinking about how to get their pawns moving.

1.Qxb7 is a poor move: after 1...Qxb7 2.Bxb7 Rab8, the white bishop must retreat, allowing Rxb2, when Black has been presented with a ready-made passed pawn on the c-file. Marshall played **1.Rfc1** which Capablanca criticized as follows: 'He should have advanced his K-side pawns at once to counterbalance the advance of Black on the Q-side. White's inactivity on his strong wing took away all the chances he had of drawing the game.'

The rest of the game is a fine example of one player increasing his advantage as the other just watches: **1...Rab8 2.Qe4 Qc7 3.Rc3 b5 4.a3 c4 5.Bf3 Rfd8 6.Rd1 Rxd1 7.Bxd1 Rd8 8.Bf3 g6 9.Qc6 Qe5 10.Qe4 Qxe4 11.Bxe4 Rd1+ 12.Kg2 a5 13.Rc2 b4 14.axb4 axb4 15.Bf3 Rb1 16.Be2 b3 17.Rd2** (17.Rc3 loses to 17...Rxb2 18.Bxc4 Rc2!) **17...Rc1 18.Bd1 c3 19.bxc3 b2 20.Rxb2 Rxd1** and Black won comfortably with his extra piece. Even when White finally resigned after another 14 moves, none of his K-side pawns had moved from their positions in the diagram.

White certainly lost this game through doing nothing. Looking at it from his point of view, he must have been relucant to play 1.e4 because it would block his bishop's diagonal and perhaps also let a black rook move to d8 and d4. The alternative, however, was to sit and wait to be squeezed to death. White need not play e4 immediately, but if he does not quickly get his pawns rolling with e4 and f4, then he will never join in the game.

38 patience

Everyone recognizes the need for patience in defence: when your opponent is pushing you around and making direct threats, there is nothing to do but knuckle down to the task of patient resistance. Yet patience can also be a considerable virtue in playing an attack. If you have a firm advantage and a natural attacking plan, your opponent wants you to get on with it. He knows what you are going to do and he has prepared his defences. He cannot be sure whether they will hold or not, and not knowing adds to his misery. The longer you keep him waiting, the more you will wear down his resistance.

> When your opponent is tied up, don't loosen the knots.

If the decisive battle is bound to be fought on the K-side, probe a little on the other wing first. Especially when you have an endgame advantage, it may pay to explore some second-rate winning plans before committing yourself to the natural and correct one. Your opponent will be psychologically prepared to meet your best plan, so why not keep him waiting? You may even find sometimes that he kills himself in frustration, trying to break out in an unjustified manner, thus saving you the trouble of winning the game altogether.

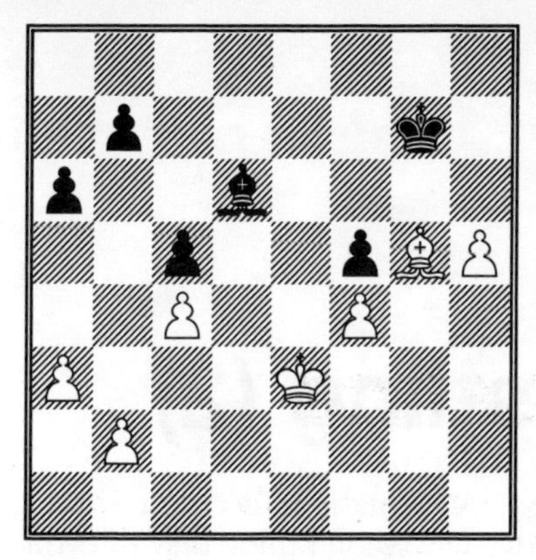

Confessions of a misspent youth, No. 2: White to play (from Hartston–Barcza, Hastings 1972–3). Can you find a winning plan?

I certainly couldn't, when my game was adjourned in the diagram position, but the experienced Czech grandmaster Vlastimil Hort helped me out. When I showed him the position and explained that the pawns on c5 and f5 effectively prevent my king from entering the black position he gave me some advice. 'You must manoeuvre,' he said. 'How?' I asked. 'It doesn't matter how,' he explained. 'Just manoeuvre.' And when I still looked quizzical, he added: 'Just go round in circles. Barcza is an old man. Keep him working, then do something at the end of the session. It doesn't matter what you do. He will go wrong.'

So on resumption, I 'manoeuvred' my king first to d3, then to g3, then along the second rank to d2 and c3. I played b3 and then b4. I brought the king to b3, a4 and a5, knowing he would only chase it back with Bc7+. I played Ka4, then pushed the pawn to b5. Then I brought the king back to f3 and exchanged pawns on a6.

After 25 moves, the only change from the diagram position was that the two b-pawns had vanished from the board. It was nearly 11pm – time to do something. The game then continued 1.Kf3 Kh7 2.Kg3 Kg7 3.Kh4 Kh7 4.Bd8! This was my only idea and he fell for it: 4...Bxf4? (4...Kh6! holds the draw – as he would surely have found if posed the problem two hours earlier. Now, with the f4 square unblocked, White has real winning prospects.) 5.Be7 Be3 6.Bg5! Bf2+ 7.Kh3 Kg7 8.Kg2 Bd4 9.Kf3 Be5 10.Bf4! Bf6 11.Bd6 Bg5 (11...Bd4 12.Kf4 Kf6 13.h6 wins for White) 12.Bxc5 Kh6 13.Bb6 Kxh5 14.c5 Be7 15.Kf4 Kg6 16.Ke5 Bf6+ 17.Ke6 Bd4 18.Ba7 Bxc5 19.Bxc5 a5 20.a4 f4. Now considerable delicacy is required to keep Black from reaching a drawn a-pawn and wrong-coloured bishop endgame: 21.Bb6 f3 22.Bd4 Kg5 23.Kd6 Kf5 24.Kd5! Kf4 25.Kc5 Ke4 26.Kc4! Kf5 27.Kb5 Ke6 28.Kxa5 Kd7 29.Kb6 Kc8 30.Ka7 resigns.

castling (2)

The first thing you're told about castling is to do it quickly to tuck your king up nice and safe. The second thing they tell you is not to rush with it all that much, because keeping your options open may keep your opponent guessing about where your king is going to end up. The third law of castling, however, renders the other two obsolete:

> Castling is a rook move.

Just think about what castling does. It's not just a case of tucking your king away; it also connects the rooks. By castling, you have committed both your rooks to the same side of the king. Sometimes you castle because it is imperative to get your king out of the centre, but when the centre is closed and likely, in the short term at least, to remain so, the right moment to castle is when you need to bring your rook into the game along the back rank – or at least when you have decided which side of the board your rooks will be needed.

When you castle, you do not only get your king away from the wide open spaces on one side of the board; you also put your rooks in touch with those same wide open spaces. Think aggressively: castling is a rook move!

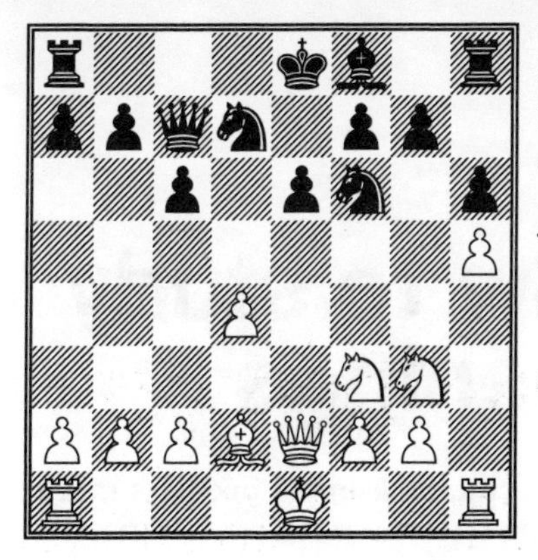

White to play in a standard variation of the Caro–Kann Defence. Where should both sides put their kings?

Just look at the way play developed in four grandmaster games.

a 1.0-0-0 0-0-0 2.Ne5 Nb6 3.Ba5 Rd5 4.Bxb6 axb6 5.c4 Rd8 6.Ne4 Nxe4 7.Qxe4 Bd6 (Spassky–Pomar, Palma de Majorca 1968).

b 1.0-0-0 c5!? 2.c4 cxd4 3.Nxd4 Bc5 4.Nb5 Qc6 5.Nf5 0-0 (Velikov–Bagirov, Wroclaw 1976).

c 1.c4 0-0-0 2.c5! Rg8 3.b4! g6 4.Rb1 gxh5 5.Kf1 Rg4 6.Rb3 (Hort–Karpov, Ljubljana 1975).

d 1.c4 Bd6 2.Nf5 0-0 3.Nxd6 Qxd6 4.Rh4 b5 (Lanka–Kasparov, USSR 1977).

In version (**a**), both players continued routinely with Q-side castling. In (**b**), Black was a little more subtle, responding to White's Q-side castling by opening lines on that flank, then castling K-side himself in order to put his rooks on c8 and d8.

In (**c**), it is White who waits and as soon as Black castles long, he decides at least one rook belongs on the Q-side to support a general advance of the pawns. The king goes to f1 because the other rook is perfectly well developed on the h-file.

In (**d**), Black castles K-side quickly, reasoning that if White is to attack him there, he will need a rook on the g-file to support an advance of the g-pawn, but that would mean that White must castle Q-side, where Black is ready to open lines for his own attack with b5.

The modern tendency in this position is for both sides to keep their castling options open for as long as possible. Players with an aggressive mentality (as White or Black) wait for their opponents to castle, then plan how to castle on the opposite wing for an attacking game; more cautious souls wait for their opponents to castle then copy them, aiming for a quiet, positional game.

40 how to study openings

Most players spend far too much time *learning* openings rather than *studying* them. An opening system is not a set of variations to be learnt by rote. It is a scheme of development connected to a set of strategies, that may carry through into the endgame.

You should choose what openings to play by looking at grandmaster games and picking those systems in which you find it natural to identify with the moves of one side. When you have found such an opening, play as many complete games in that opening as you can find. Then play them all through quickly.

You will need at least a dozen games, and ideally something closer to a hundred. You will almost certainly find, as you start playing through the games, that some of the early moves look unnatural to you. A knight wanders off to the edge of the board when you would have been inclined to centralize it; or a player castles Q-side when the other wing looks more natural to you; or a pawn weakness is suddenly allowed for no apparent reason.

After a dozen games, however, you find that similar manoeuvres crop up again and again. When you started they felt like strange words in a foreign language; by game 20 they have become part of your commonplace vocabulary. And after 30 of 40 games, you find yourself correctly guessing the vast majority of the moves.

> Then is the time – and not before – to start looking up the opening in a theoretical manual.

Just learning variations will never enable you to develop a proper feel for a particular opening. In very sharp openings, of course, where both players may be skating on a knife edge of tactics, some precise knowledge is indispensable. In practice, however, you will do well to avoid complex and fashionable systems. It's just too easy to lose without having joined in the game at all.

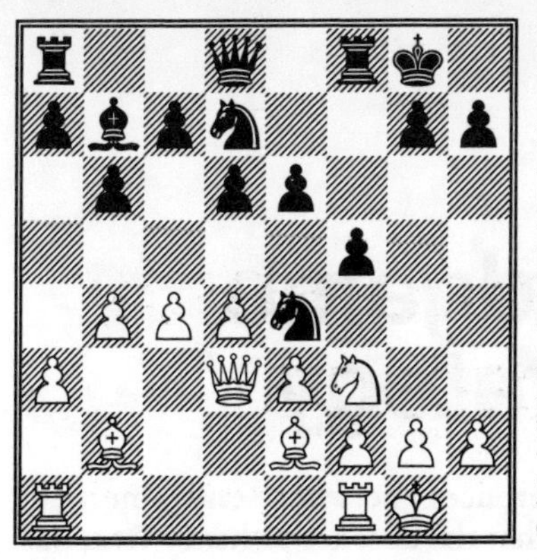

This position, reached after the moves 1.d4 Nf6 2.c4 e6 3.Nf3 Bb4+ 4.Nbd2 b6 5.a3 Bxd2+ 6.Qxd2 Bb7 7.e3 0-0 8.Be2 d6 9.0-0 Nbd7 10.b4 Ne4 11.Qd3 f5 12.Bb2, led to one of the most startling defeats of a top grandmaster in recent years. Boris Gelfand, playing White against Miguel Illescas at Madrid 1996, played a series of natural enough moves but did not survive as far as move 20. It was all due to a deep failure of his understanding of the opening.

Countless games from positions similar to that of the diagram have established the various ways play may progress: Black can play Qe7 and e5 to fight for central space (the usual plan), or he can try g5 and g4 for a K-side attack (a plan that generally creates too many weaknesses in his own king's defences), or he can try an alternative attacking plan with Rf6 and Rg6 or Rh6. White can play for c5, opening lines on the Q-side, or d5, blocking the black bishop out of the game and freeing d4 for the white knight, or he can try Ne1 and f3 to expel the knight from e4. Those are the ideas. Now watch how the game went.

12...Rf6!? 13.d5 Rg6! (After 12...e5 13.Nh4! the tactical threat of Nxf5 and positional threat of f4 and Nf3 give Black severe problems.) **14.dxe6** (A decision taken too lightly. After blocking the long diagonal with d5, White should be reluctant to open it again. 14.Ne1 or 14.Nd4!? are more in keeping with the position.) **14...Nf8! 15.c5?** (With Black's rook on g6, knight on e4 and bishop on b7 all aggressively placed, and the other knight now on course for e6 and g5, this is no time for White to be fiddling around on the Q-side. 15.Ne1 was imperative.) **15...Nxe6 16.cxd6 cxd6 17.Rad1 Kh8 18.Ne1** (now too late) **18...N6g5! 19.Kh1** (the threat was 19...Nh3+ 20.Kh1 Nexf2+) **19...Nh3!! White resigned.** 20.gxh3 Nxf2 is mate, and nothing else can defend against the threatened Nexf2+.

A disaster for White, who played as though Black's entire attacking scheme came as a total surprise to him.

4 endgame strategy

There are two great differences between endgame and middlegame play: the first is that the absence of heavy weapons from the board in the endgame lets the kings play an active part; the second, and far more radical difference, however, is in the manner in which one assesses positions. For most of the middlegame one's thoughts are wandering about in a fog of 'White stands a little better' or 'Black has good attacking chances'. As the endgame approaches, however, one moves gradually towards definite assessments of win, loss or draw.

Every player builds through experience a personal library of types of position on which definite judgements may be made. Almost all king and pawn endgames, most opposite-coloured bishop endgames, the majority of positions in which one player has the advantage of the last remaining pawn on the board: they are all on the list of positions one must try to work out.

> More half-points are thrown away by the inability to recognize a technically won endgame than through any other single cause.

A great part of the art of good endgame play lies in recognizing when 'better' turns to 'winning' and when 'difficult' turns to 'lost'. One of the defects of early computer chess programs was their poor endgame play – caused largely by their reliance on a 'positional evaluation function' which told you, with spurious authority, that White had an advantage of +174 or somesuch figure. Chess would be a far duller game if it were possible to design a function so that +174 was a draw but +175 was a win. Such a mathematical model may simulate good middlegame play, but the endgame exposes its deficiencies. Many human players exhibit the same failing of thinking in degrees of 'better' and 'worse' when their evaluation functions should have moved on to the discrete 'win', 'loss' or 'draw'.

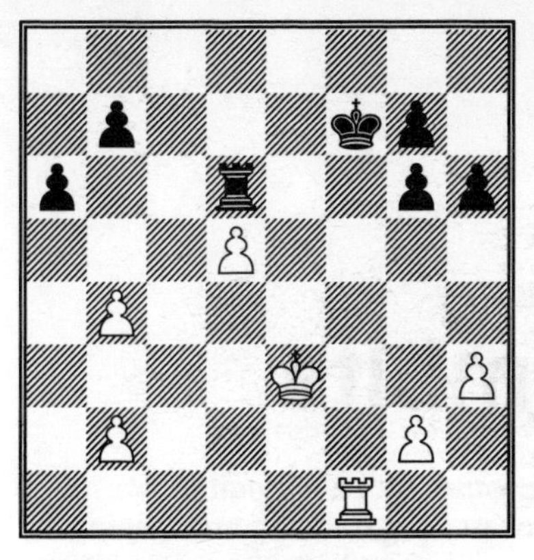

Black to play in Botvinnik–Flohr, USSR Championship 1944. Should he escape from check by moving his king or interpose his rook?

Black is clearly worse: his doubled g-pawns prevent him from obtaining a passed pawn, so White's d-pawn acts almost as an extra pawn. After 1...Ke7 2.Kd4 Rb6 3.Kc5 Rb5+ 4.Kc4, Black can only wait to see if White can win the game since 4...Kd6 is ineffective in view 5.Rf8. It is tempting to reason that 1...Rf6 can be no worse, since 2.Rxf6+ will straighten out Black's pawns, but the logic is faulty. 1...Ke7 gives chances of a draw; 1...Rf6 loses. Here's what happened in the game.

1...Rf6 2.Rxf6+ gxf6 3.g4! Ke7 4.h4 Kd6 5.Ke4 b6 6.h5! gxh5 7.gxh5 a5 8.Kf5! axb4 9.Kxf6 Kxd5 10.Kg6 Ke6 (Running to take the b-pawn is too slow.) **11.Kxh6 Kf6 12.b3 Kf7 13.Kg5 Kg7 14.Kf5 Kh6 15.Ke5 Kxh5 16.Kd5 Kg5 17.Kc6 Kf5 18.Kxb6 Ke6 19.Kc5 Kd7 20.Kxb4 Kc6 21.Ka5 Kb7 22.Kb5 Ka7 23.Kc6 Ka6 24.b4 Ka7 25.b5 Kb8 26.Kb6 resigns.**

'But that's 26 moves past the diagram,' I hear you protest. 'How can I be expected to see that far?' In fact, it ought not to be so difficult. After 2.Rxf6+ gxf6, the move 3.g4! is the natural way to give Black problems in utilizing his newly freed pawn majority. He can only create a passed pawn by playing ...f5, when White has the natural plan of giving up d-pawn for f-pawn, leaving his own king ready to move to g6 and capture on h6. The rest is just a matter of counting and establishing that Black cannot create a sufficiently advanced pawn of his own while White is playing Kg6, Kxh6 and queening the h-pawn.

Now go back to the diagram and nudge the black pawn back from h6 to h7. What happens then after 1...Rf6 2.Rxf6+ gxf6? This time it's a draw, because after 3.g4 Ke7, White can no longer force an entry on the K-side with h4 and h5. Black just ignores the pawn when it reaches h5. If White wants to play for a win, he must avoid the exchange of rooks and try 2.Rc1 instead.

gambits

From the Italian: *gamba*, a leg; *gambetto*, a leg-pull in wrestling to trip up the opponent. In chess, a gambit is an opening in which one player sacrifices material, usually a pawn, in order to gain the initiative. In the 19th century, when the emphasis was firmly on all-out attacking play, gambits were all the rage. Pawns were thrown away as excess ballast just to let one's pieces engage the enemy more quickly.

Gradually, as defensive technique came to be understood, the gambits had their teeth drawn. In every case, methods were found either to keep the extra pawn and survive the attack, or to return the extra pawn to obtain a comfortable game. Now, you will scarcely find a top-class player who engages in gambit play other than as an occasional change from more sober openings.

World champions will play the Queen's Gambit, which isn't a gambit at all – if it is accepted, White may regain the pawn by force. Garry Kasparov will occasionally play the Evans Gambit – against selected openings, chosen for their dislike of defending. David Bronstein would play the King's Gambit, just to prove that the spirit of romance is not yet dead. Other strong grandmasters will chance the Benko Gambit as a calculatedly risky way of winning games as Black against inferior opposition.

Under normal circumstances, however, strong players appreciate the value of a pawn. Anyone who throws one away willingly in the first few moves ought to realize that he is committing an offence against the natural laws of the game.

A pawn is a pawn.

Giving them away is not a good habit to get into – unless you're just pulling someone's leg.

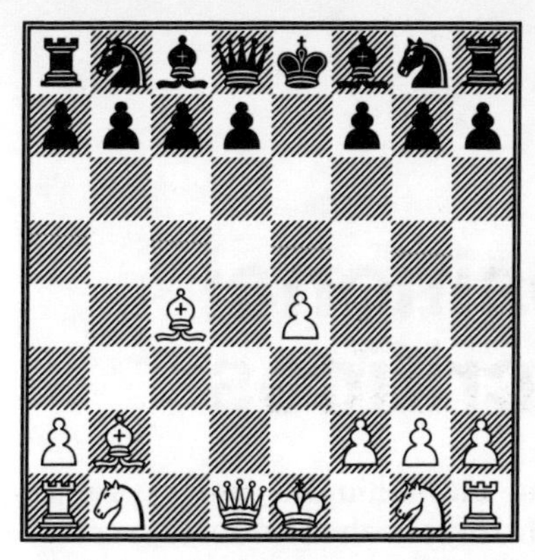

The characteristic position of the Danish Gambit, reached after the moves 1.e4 e5 2.d4 exd4 3.c3 dxc3 4.Bc4 cxb2 5.Bb2. White has two bishops posted aggressively before Black has even begun his development. How should Black react?

The line that really put the Danish Gambit out of commission was 5...d5 6.Bxd5 (After 6.exd5 Nf6 Black is out of danger on the c4–f7 diagonal and can complete his development in peace, remaining a pawn ahead for nothing.) 6...Nf6 7.Bxf7+! (Otherwise Nxd5 leaves Black with a clear advantage.) 7...Kxf7 8.Qxd8 Bb4+. Black regains his queen and has rather the better of the endgame. That, however, is rather a tactical solution to the problem. More typical anti-gambit play was seen in the games Mieses–Maroczy, Monte Carlo 1902 which went, from the diagram: **5...d6 6.Ne2 Nc6 7.0-0 Be6 8.Bd5 Nf6 9.Qb3 Qc8 10.Nf4 Bxd5 11.exd5 Ne5! 12.Re1 Be7** (Black systematically reduces White's initiative by returning his extra material.) **13.Bxe5 dxe5 14.Rxe5 Qd7! 15.Qg3** (Since 15.Qxb7 0-0 would leave White in considerable disarray, he tries his luck on the other wing.) **15...0-0-0! 16.Qxg7 Qd6! 17.Qg5** (17.Rf5 would have been met by 17...Qb4! With the double threat of Qe1 mate and Qb2.) **17...Rfe8 18.Nd2** (There was nothing better.) **18...Nd7 19.Rxe7 Qxe7**. Now Black is winning and the game ended with **20.Qg3 Qb4 21.Nf3 Rg8 22.Qh4 Qc3 23.Rb1 Qxf3 White resigned.**

That's the real trouble with gambits: when you're a pawn or two down to start with, winning a pawn or two only restores material equality. And then you find you're worse off because of the time you lost regaining your pawns.

43 positional sacrifices

One important step up from old-fashioned gambits on the evolutionary ladder of chess heroism is the positional sacrifice. Giving up a pawn for a temporary lead in development is one thing, but sacrificing material for long-term positional gains is a concept of a higher order.

There are two types of positional sacrifice worth mentioning for their frequency of occurrence.

- *The wing-pawn sacrifice:* where a pawn is used as bait to lure an enemy pawn away from the centre. In the Benko Gambit, for example, after 1.d4 Nf6 2.c4 c5 3.d5, Black plays 3...b5 4.cxb5 a6. The sacrifice will open the a- and b-files for Black's rooks, while also allowing Black to consider undermining operations in the centre with ...e6 or even ...f5.
- *The exchange sacrifice*: where a rook is surrendered for a bishop or knight to create pawn weaknesses and the type of position in which a minor piece may function more effectively than a rook. These are commonly seen in the Sicilian Defence, with Black playing ...Rxc3 to wreck the defences around a Q-side castled white king, or White playing h4 and h5, and meeting Nxh5 with Rxh5 to shatter the pawn shield round the black king.

All these examples have one thing in common:

A positional sacrifice is designed to change the character of the game.

It creates outposts for pieces where they previously had none; it creates open files for previously inactive rooks; it denies the opponent important attacking options. Finally, there is the psychological impact: the greatest effect of the positional sacrifice may be to remove the initiative from a player who thought he had everything under control. In many cases, that alone will be sufficient value.

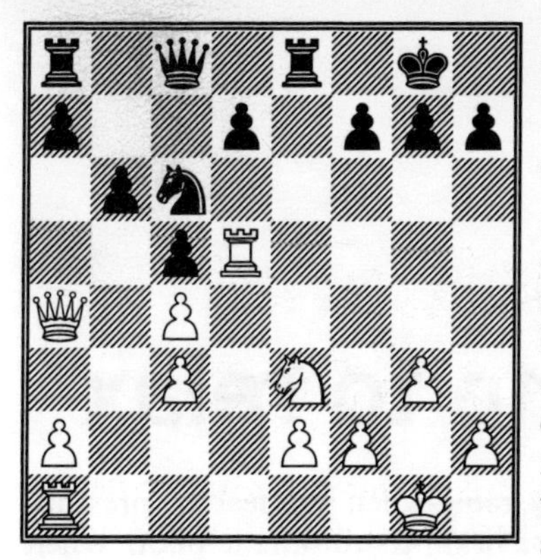

Black to play in Benko–Keres, Los Angeles 1963. Who stands better?

White's c-pawns are a potential weakness, but he seems to have all the play. By doubling rooks on the d-file, he will tie Black down to defending d7. Meanwhile he can also consider shifting the rook to g5 or h5 and bringing the knight to d5 or f5 for a K-side attack. Black's own knight can attack c4 and defend d7 from e5, but will always have to reckon on being kicked back when White plays f4.

Keres decided this was the moment to join in the game and played **1...Rxe3! 2.fxe3 Qe8**. Suddenly, the game is transformed. If White defends e3 with 3.Kf2, then 3...Qe6 followed by Re8 leaves him in a desperate mess. Quite apart from the attack on e3, there are threats of a huge attack with Qh3 and Ne5. The game continued **3.Qc2 Qxe3+ 4.Kh1 Ne5 5.Rf1 Re8 6.Rf4 f6**. With a pawn for the exchange and a knight beautifully anchored at e5, Black had full value for his sacrifice. After **7.Qe4?** (7.Rd1 is much better) **7...Ng6! 8.Qxe3 Rxe3** White was already in grave difficulties. Liking neither 9.Rf3 Rxe2 10.Rxd7 Ne5 11.Rd8+ Kf7 nor 9.Rf2 Ne5, he decided to return the material with **9.Rxd7 Nxf4 10.gxf4 Rxe2 11.Rxa7**, but after **11...Rf2 12.Rb7 Rxf4 13.Rxb6 Rxc4** Black's pawn advantage was enough to win.

The interesting thing is that White's move prior to the diagram position had been with his knight from g2 to e3. Had he seen even a glimmer of what was about to happen, he would instead have defended e2 by playing Qc2, when White has every chance of advantage.

44 time to relax

There come moments in every game when you feel the pressure is off and you can switch your brain to automatic pilot. When you have been under pressure and finally forced your opponent's attacking pieces to retreat, or when you have simplified to a winning endgame a couple of pawns ahead, you breathe a sigh of relief and congratulate yourself on your patience and skill. You make a mental note that when you come to annotate this particular encounter in your 'Best Games' collection, this is the move when you will write: '... and the rest is just technique.'

Then you lean back in your chair and make the fatal blunder. For this is the moment when most games are thrown away.

> The easiest time to blunder is the move after you have solved all the difficult problems.

From proper hard thinking, you begin to rely on general principles, forgetting how unprincipled they can be. It has been said that chess is the only area of human activity where paranoia is a positive advantage. Actually there are many such areas, but chess is one where an element of paranoia is an occupational necessity. Every move and every position has to be viewed with mistrust. Once you find yourself thinking: 'Nothing can go wrong now' you have set up the preconditions for something to go wrong. And, as Grandmaster Murphy pointed out: if anything can go wrong, it will.

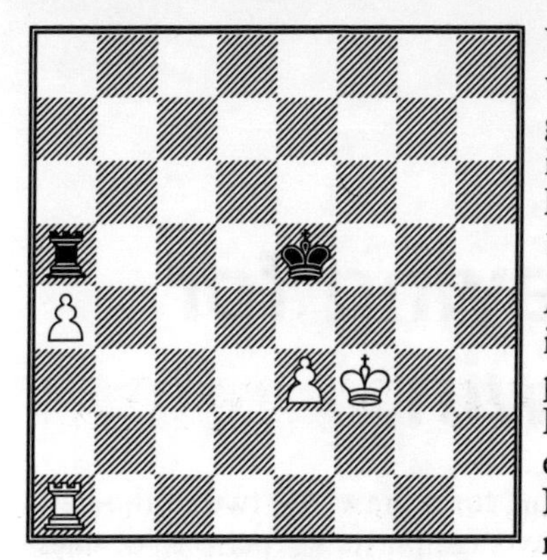

White to play and throw the win away; Black to reply and give it straight back. (An infamous endgame from the Kasparov–Short match of 1993.)

After catching his opponent in a spectacularly venomous piece of opening preparation, Kasparov reached this endgame two pawns ahead. Now as everyone knows, rook and two pawns always wins against rook, except in a handful of well-documented cases. Neither player seemed to disagree with that assessment, and the game reached its logical conclusion after **1.e4 Ke6 2.Ke3 Kd6 3.Kd4 Kd7 4.Kc4 Kc6 5.Kb4 Re5 6.Rc1+ Kb6 7.Rc4,** and Black resigned. The white king ambles back towards d4 and shepherds the e-pawn home.

So what was wrong with that? Only that 1.e4?? was a terrible blunder, giving Black the chance to escape with a draw by means of 1...Rc5! After 2.Ra3 (to prevent the check on c3) 2...Rc4! 3.a5 Rxe4 4.a6, Black's rook rushes back with Rf4+, Rf8 and Ra8 to save the draw, while after 2.a5 Rc3+ 3.Kg4 Kxe4 4.a6 Rc8 5.a7 Ra8 6.Ra5 Black escapes by the skin of his teeth with 6...Kd4 7.Kf5 Kc4 8.Ke6 Kb4 9.Ra1 Kc5 10.Kd7 Kb6 11.Rb1+ Kc5! (not 11...Kxa7? 12.Kc7 when White wins at once) 12.Rb7 Rh8! and White can make no progress.

White's casual 1.e4?? was perfectly mirrored by Black's 1...Ke6?? Both players had mentally written the game off as a win for White, and neither believed that anything could go wrong. Instead of this nonsense, 1.Ra3! wins for White without great difficulty.

45 playing for a win

'Playing for a win' and 'playing for a draw' are two of the most overused expressions in the average player's repertoire of chess clichés. 'Playing for a draw' is what your opponent was doing when he exchanged all your pieces before you could think of a way to launch an attack. 'Playing for a win' is either what you were doing when you wrecked your own position through overboldness or a phrase you incorporate into a draw offer ('Are you playing for a win?') to imply that your opponent has no moral right to continue the game.

Occasionally you may be faced with a genuine choice between a line that simplifies to a probable draw and a move that enters unfathomable complications. Under such circumstances, you may legitimately ask yourself whether you are playing for a win or a draw. Most of the time, however, an inner conviction that you are 'playing for a win' has no effect other than to interfere with your objectivity. There is a Zen saying that the archer who aims for the bullseye will win the prize, but one who sets his sights on the prize will miss the target. It's the same in chess.

> **The man who plays for a win or a draw will lose; the one who looks for the best moves will win.**

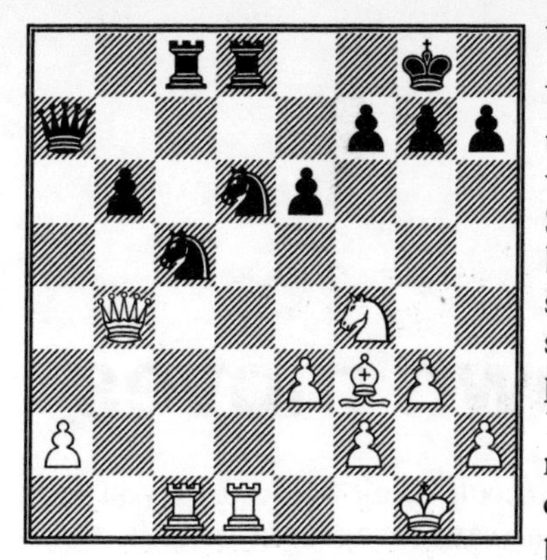

White to play ... for a win!

When Garry Kasparov came to the final game of his match with Anatoly Karpov in Seville in 1987, he was a point behind and needed to win to save his title. As White under such circumstances, most players would open 1.e4 or 1.d4, and choose the sharpest, most aggressive opening they could imagine. Kasparov played 1.c4, 2.Nf3, 3.g3 and 4.b3 – his least aggressive opening play of the entire match.

The logic was simple: he was not looking for the sort of flashy initiative that might be dissipated with time; what he wanted was a small but enduring advantage. The sort of thing that would let him play on and on, forever nagging away at an anxious opponent.

The result, after 22 moves, was the diagram position. If the a-pawn and b-pawn are exchanged, the game will surely be drawn, but after Kasparov's **23.a3!** White had a tiny edge. Thanks to his bishop's control of a8, Black will find it difficult to build up pressure against a3, while White can hope to add to his own attack against b6. It will not be enough to win the pawn, but might force Black onto the defensive.

Now watch what followed: **23...Nf5 24.Rb1 Rxd1+ 25.Rxd1 Qc7 26.Nd3! h6 27.Rc1 Ne7 28.Qb5 Nf5 29.a4! Nd6 30.Qb1 Qa7 31.Ne5! Nxa4** (Later analysis suggested that 31...Qxa4 32.Qxb6 Qa3! 33.Rd1 Nce4! might have been a better defence.) **32.Rxc8+ Nxc8 33.Qd1** (33.Qb5! was more accurate) **33...Ne7?** (Black had to find 33...Nc5! when 34.Qd8+ Kh7 35.Qxc8? Qa1+! is bad for Black, though 35.Bd1! is quite unclear.) **34.Qd8+ Kh7 35.Nxf7 Ng6 36.Qe8 Qe7 37.Qxa4 Qxf7 38.Be4 Kg8 39.Qb5 Nf8 40.Qxb6** and White eventually won with his extra pawn.

The point of all this is not the complex variations hinted at in the above notes. It is that Kasparov judged that he could 'play for a win' even in a position as simplified and apparently dull as that of the diagram. And events proved him totally correct.

46 pawn moves

Pawn moves are the most difficult of all because, as you may have been told already, pawns cannot move backwards. Once the pawn structure has begun to take shape, the possible patterns of play are determined. Each side wants to increase his control of space, and the way to take over space is to advance your pawns systematically. But every pawn advance leaves weak squares behind it. There is always a danger, when you are gaily storming ahead with your pawns, that your opponent's pieces will outflank you by slipping behind your advancing infantry.

> Never push a pawn without giving a thought to the squares it leaves unprotected.

In the majority of positions, the entire strategy is effectively determined by the pawns. They are the men you use to push the enemy back and to open lines for your attack, but they need proper support of the pieces behind them. The pawn structure itself determines which are the good pawn moves that you should be aiming to carry out in the medium term, and which are the bad pawn moves that should be avoided unless they bring immediate gains. But even the best pawn moves may need a good deal of preparation.

Passed pawns, said Nimzowitsch, have a lust to expand. Indeed every pawn, however impotent it may look in a given position, harbours a similar lust. However, lust is not something we should allow ourselves to get carried away with.

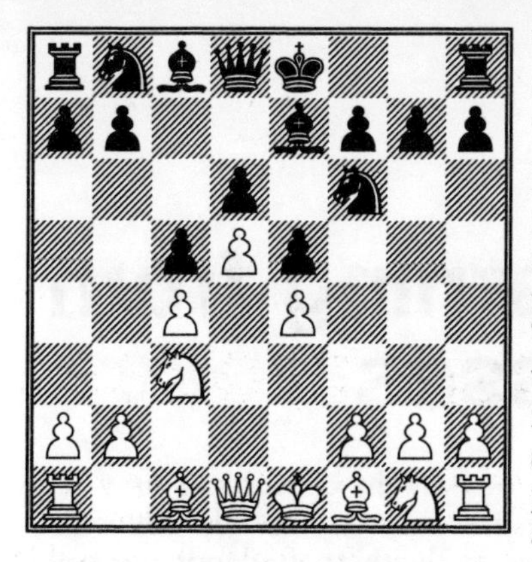

White to move. What are the important decisions to be taken concerning pawn play?

Looking at Black's strategy first: his pawns on e5 and c5 indicate that he should be trying to advance f5 and b5. The first requires support with ...g6 (so that a pawn may recapture on f5); the second envisages some such plan as Na6, Nc7, Bd7, a6 and b5.

White would like to get rid of the pawns on e5 and c5 to give his own e-pawn and c-pawn the chance of joining the d-pawn on the fifth-rank. Now consider the move 1.f4, which is a surprisingly common choice in this position by club players. The move should ring alarm bells, since 1...exf4 leaves the white e-pawn backward and a fine potential outpost for a black knight at e5. White's 1.f4 is only justifiable if, after 1...exf4 2.Bxf4, he is sure he will be able to play a quick e5. In fact, after 2...Nbd7 3.Nf3 (renewing the e5 threat), Black can play 3...Nh5, chasing the bishop from f4 and holding back the e-pawn.

Instead of 1.f4?! White has three good strategies. One is to play 1.g3 and aim for a later f4 when his exf4 can be met by gxf4. The second is simply to get on with his development with Nf3, Be2 and 0-0 while preparing a Q-side line-opening pawn advance with a3 and b4. The third is to restrain Black on the K-side with Bd3, h3 and g4, hoping to hold up ...f5 and increase White's space advantage.

A typical continuation might be **1.Nf3 0-0 2.Be2 Ne8** (freeing the way for the f-pawn to advance later) **3.0-0 Nbd7 4.a3** (preparing b4) **4...g6** (the necessary pawn move to prepare f5) **5.Bh6 Ng7 6.Qd2** (in order to meet f5 with Ng5! Note how Black's f5 leaves the e6 square without a strong guard.) **6...Kh8 7.b4 b6** (to meet bxc5 with bxc5, keeping the centre firm). Black will continue with Nf6 and Ng8 to expel the bishop from h6; White will play Ne1 and prepare for the right moment to open the game with f4.

4 learning from losses

There are two main schools of thought concerning how one should react to defeats. The one most commonly advocated involves analysing your losses in depth to find out not only where you went wrong, but why you went wrong, so that you may avoid losing again for the same reasons. The one most commonly practised, however, is to blame the lighting, your state of health, atmospheric conditions or any other off-the-board incident in order to exculpate yourself from any suggestion that the loss might in any way have been *your* fault.

If you want to eradicate your weaknesses, there are still two ways to set about it. When you have lost a game, your job is not just to identify the error but to discover what it was about the position that led to your making the error. Were you perhaps too bold in a position that demanded caution? Did you lack the courage to play the right move because you could not analyse it through to the end? Did you create too many weak squares by injudicious pawn advances?

Whatever your diagnosis, you now have a choice to make. For a quick improvement in your results, the simple solution is to avoid similar positions in the future. If you lost as Black because your white-squared bishop was such a useless piece in the endgame, the answer is simple: give up the French Defence and Dutch Defence. No more bad bishops. In the long term, especially if you have real ambitions to become a stronger player, you have to learn how to handle such positions.

> Successful players avoid positions they do not understand; but true strength is acquired only by studying such positions until you do understand them.

One hundred French Defences of Mikhail Botvinnik will teach you everything you need to know about bad bishops.

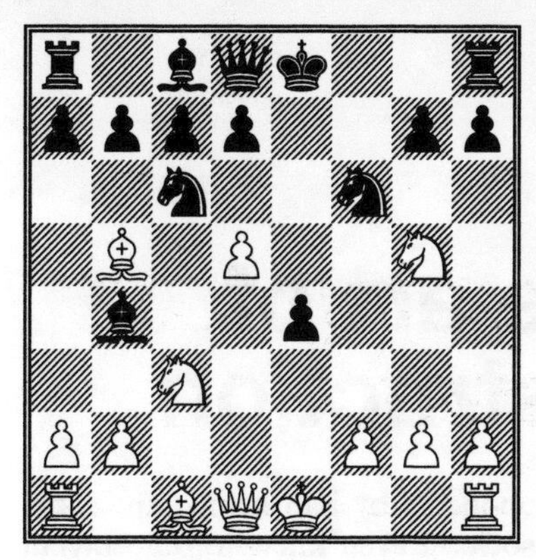

Black to play and lose in one – from Levens–Thomas, British Championship 1963.

A.R.B. Thomas (the A stood for Andrew, but he was one of those gentlemen of the old school who were always better known by their initials) was a strong county player in the 1950s and 1960s, on the fringe of the British team. He might have been an even better player if he had shown greater ability to learn from his defeats. This is a particularly drastic example.

The diagram position was reached after the following moves: 1.e4 e5 2.Nf3 Nc6 3.Bb5 Bc5 (the Classical Defence to the Ruy Lopez – a lifelong favourite of Thomas's) 4.c3 f5 5.d4 exd4 (5...fxe4 is more usual) 6.cxd4 (and here 6.e5 is more testing) 6...Bb4+ 7.Nc3 fxe4 8.Ng5 Nf6 9.d5. Now, after some thought, Black retreated his attacked knight with **9...Ne7??** and resigned after **10.Ne6!**

A rare smothered mate of the queen, you might think, aided by a pin on the d-pawn. Thomas's comment as he congratulated his opponent, however, suggested that such an occurrence may not be so rare after all: 'That's the third time I've lost my queen that way,' he said with a rueful smile.

As Lady Bracknall might have said; 'To lose one queen, Mr Thomas, may be regarded as a misfortune; to lose three looks like a chronic inability to learn from experience.' Make sure that the reasons for your losses remain engraved on your mind deeply enough to ring warning bells whenever a similar losing opportunity arises.

48 the art of distraction

Some players distract their opponents by bad behaviour at the board, or by wearing garish socks. I even knew a Yugoslavian master once who mastered the trick of getting into time-trouble then rushing off to pay an obviously urgent visit to the toilet – all to get the opponent to rush one vital move. We are not concerned with such distracting tactics here. Legitimate distraction involves distracting not your opponent but his pieces.

Beginners' games are decided by simple oversights – unforced errors that earn immediate punishment. The second stage of any player's development is learning how to tempt errors by making threats. If your opponent will not lose the game on his own, then you need to create some opportunities for him to do so. You create a weakness and plug away at it until your opponent wilts.

But what do you do if he doesn't wilt? The answer is that you move on to stage three: winning by distraction. One weakness in the opponent's position may not be enough. You attack it, your opponent defends it; result: deadlock. And that is the time to create another front for your attack. Emotionally, this is one of the most difficult lessons to learn. Your natural inclination may be to keep on plugging away in the area of the board where you are doing well. Yet the way to win will often be to launch an attack on the other wing. Your opponent's men, distracted by defensive duties, will then be unable to cope with problems on both wings. The message is simple:

Don't play in blinkers.

A high-class game is rarely a simple progression down a single track. Do not be disappointed if the first wave of your attack does not reap the desired benefits. It may well be enough for it to have distracted your opponent's men away from an area where nothing much seems to be happening now, yet will prove to be the site of the decisive battle.

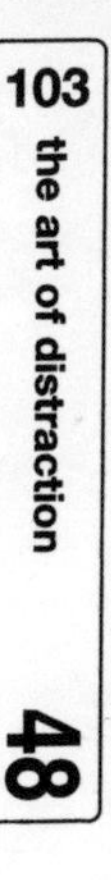

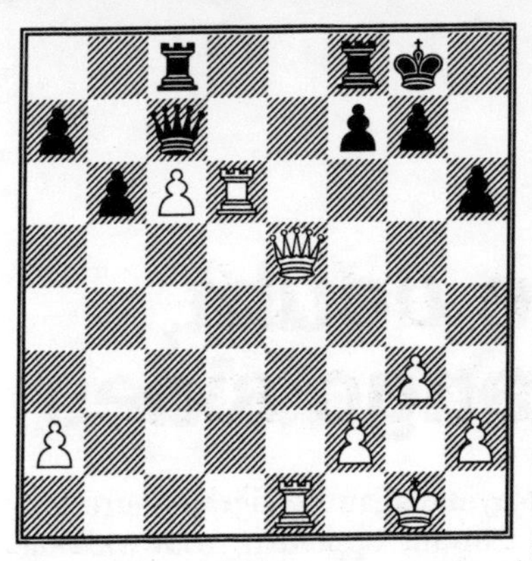

From Petrosian–Korchnoi, Candidates' match 1977. White to play. How can he utilize the advantage of his passed c-pawn?

When you have laboured long and hard to create such a pawn, your thoughts may easily become fixated on how to force it forward still further. Here's how your thoughts might well go: 'I've got to dislodge his queen from c7, and the way to do that must be by playing Rd7 sometime. When I do that, I'll need something else to defend c6, so 1.Rc1 looks like a good idea. It even sets a trap, because if he plays 1...Rcd8, I have 2.Rxd8! Qxe5 (2...Qxd8 3.c7 must be very strong for White) 3.Rxf8+ Kxf8 4.c7! and my pawn forces its way home.' Now watch how Petrosian handled the position.

1.Qd5! Kh7 (1...Rfd8 is met by 2.Rd7!) **2.Re4!** (Far stronger than 2.Rc1, when Black plays 2...Rcd8 3.Rd7 Rxd7 4.Qxd7 and now either 4...Rc8 or 4...Qxd7 5.cxd7 Rd8 gives Black every chance of a draw.) **2...Kg8 3.Kg2 a6 4.h4! b5 5.g4!** (The pawns advance to create a second front on the K-side. With Black's queen and rook distracted by their Q-side duties, White will win by attack on the other wing.) **Kh7 6.Re2 Kh8 7.g5! h5** (Black must try to keep the position closed. If the h-file becomes open, his king will soon feel the draught.) **8.Rd2 Rfe8 9.Qf3 g6 10.R2d5 Rf8 11.Rf6 Qe7 12.Rd7 Qe8 13.Rxg6! Qe5** (13...fxg6 14.Qc3+ leads to mate.) **14.Qxh5 mate.**

if in doubt, change sides

When Bobby Fischer was playing against Tigran Petrosian once, he asked the referee to stop his opponent from walking round behind him and looking at the position from over his shoulder. A psychologist might interpret such behaviour as a symptom of a paranoid fear of invasion of personal space, but a good chess player knows that there is far more to it.

Looking at the position from your opponent's point of view is a good way to avoid being lured into subjectivity. You don't actually need to get up and look over your opponent's shoulder (though such a routine may help to break concentration for long enough to let new ideas in); it is enough just to wonder, occasionally, what the position looks like from the other side of the board.

Players agree draws in better positions because they do not spare a thought for the problems of the other side. They fail to play an obviously strong move because they cannot analyse it clearly enough. They accept weaknesses just to lessen the tension in the position, without realizing that the tension was worrying the opponent just as much.

If you feel your courage wilting, try mentally swapping sides and ask yourself this question:

> **If I were playing the other side, what's the move I'd fear most?**

Then play it and leave your opponent to do the worrying. It's so easy, and so unnecessary, to solve your opponent's problems for him. Or not to set him any problems at all. A similar principle applies in defence too, but with an important difference. An attacker cannot be frightened, only disconcerted. A defender is frightened by direct threats; an attacker may be disconcerted by having too many options. So ask yourself: 'If I were on the other side, which move would leave me most puzzled about what to do next?'

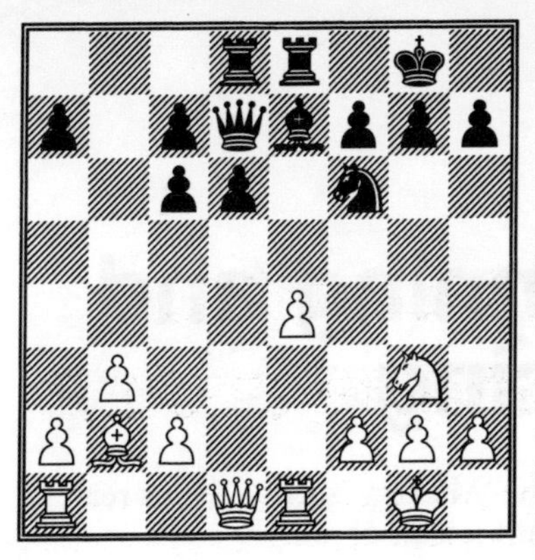

This position, from the Tarrasch–Lasker match of 1908, is a classic example of bamboozling. It is Black (Lasker) to play and he has a perfectly miserable position. He would like to fight for more space in the centre with 1...d5, but 2.e5 leaves his knight no good square to run to. Meanwhile the white knight is poised to advance to f5 and 1...g6 2.Qf3 Qe6 3.e5 leaves Black's game in ruins. Most Black players would just sit tight and wait to be engulfed by such moves as Nf5, Qf3, even c4 and Rad1, or g4 and g5. White has it all his own way.

Lasker had the idea to challenge the white bishop on the long diagonal by playing 1...Ng4. Most players' thoughts would then continue on these lines: 'After 1...Ng4, he can play 2.Nf5, attacking g7 and cutting off the defence to the knight on g4; I can probably get away with 2...Bf6 then, but instead of 2.Nf5, he can even play 2.Bxg7 when Kxg7 3.Nf5+ wins back the knight with an extra pawn for White. Terrible move; I'd better do something else.' Now watch how the game went.

1...Ng4!? 2.Bxg7 Nxf2!

Now White has a choice, and it's choices that lead to mistakes. He can win a pawn with 3.Kxf2 Kxg7 4.Nf5+ followed by Qd4 and Qxa7, or he can play for the attack with 3.Qd4. For someone who was, a moment earlier, sitting on a comfortable advantage, it is not an easy decision. And Tarrasch made the wrong choice:

3.Kxf2 Kxg7 4.Nf5+ Kh8 5.Qd4+ f6 6.Qxa7 Bf8 7.Qd4 Re5!

White is still objectively better, but he has lost his grip on the game and Black is back in the fight. After **8.Rad1 Rde8 9.Qc3 Qf7 10.Ng3 Bh6 11.Qf3 d5!** the initiative was firmly in Black's hands and after **12.exd5 Be3+ 13.Kf1 cxd5 14.Rd3?** (14.Nf5 was the right move) **14...Qe6 15.Re2 f5 16.Rd1 f4 17.Nh1 d4 18.Nf2 Qa6! 19.Nd3 Rg5 20.Ra1 Qh6** White was quite lost. 21.h3 Rg3 leaves Black threatening a winning queen sacrifice on h3, while the game continuation of **21.Ke1 Qxh2** only let White hang on for a few more moves.

50 winning and losing

Finally, before moving on to the 'Mastery' section, let us remind ourselves of the most important lesson of all:

> You don't win games by playing good moves;
> you lose them by playing bad ones.

Good moves and mistakes are inextricably linked. A good move may be needed to punish an opponent for a mistake; a good move may tempt a mistake; but good moves do not in themselves win games or even create advantages. The best they can do is put the finger on mistakes already made or set the sort of problems that lead to errors.

This is surprisingly easy to forget in the heat of battle. When your opponent comes up with a move that you have overlooked, or an idea that suddenly looks much stronger than you had previously thought it to be, it is easy to sink into gloom and assume that your position is already bad. At such moments, you may need to remind yourself that you have not yet made any mistakes, so you cannot yet stand at any disadvantage. You simply have a problem to solve. So stop moping and solve it!

This, incidentally, is one of the few times when it is a good idea to pay any attention to the past history of a position. Normally, all that should concern you is the position in front of you. How you got there is a matter of complete irrelevance. Except when you need to call the previous moves in evidence to acquit yourself of the charge of having made a mistake.

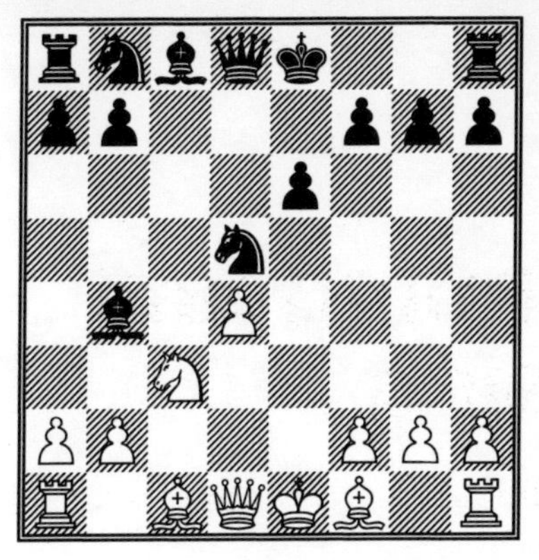

This opening position may be reached after either 1.e4 c6 2.d4 d5 3.exd5 cxd5 4.c4 e6 5.Nc3 Nf6 6.Nf3 Bb4 7.cxd5 Nxd5 or 1.d4 d5 2.c4 e6 3.Nc3 Nf6 4.Nf3 c5 5.cxd5 Nxd5 6.e3 cxd4 7.exd4 Bb4. Nowadays it is relatively common, but when Najdorf found himself in this position as White against Portisch in the Chess Olympics at Varna 1962, he had never seen it before. Reaching it by the second move order, Black's 7...Bb4 was a novelty, in place of the usual 7...Be7. With his knight attacked and not eager to commit his bishop to the rather passive post of d2, Najdorf continued **8.Qc2 Nc6 9.Bd3** and was surprised by Black's **9...Nxc3 10.bxc3 Nxd4**. His first thought, he admitted after the game, was that he had blundered away an important pawn for nothing. Since 11.Qa4+ Nc6 12.cxb4 Qxd3 is very good for Black, he continued **11.Nxd4 Qxd4** then paused to compose himself.

His reasoning followed two lines: firstly, Black has produced a new idea and won a pawn. It must therefore be a genius idea or an idiot idea. A genius is born every generation, an idiot every second, so the odds are in favour of it being an idiot idea. Secondly, *White has done nothing wrong* – his moves have been too natural to be errors, so his position cannot be bad. Having thus talked himself out of panicking, Najdorf went on to win a brilliancy: **12.Bb5+! Ke7** (12...Bd7? loses to 13.Bxd7+ Kxd7 14.Qa4+) **13.0-0! Qxc3 14.Qe2! Bd6** (14...Qxa1 loses the queen to 15.Bg5+) **15.Bb2 Qa5 16.Rfd1 Rd8 17.Qh5 f6 18.Qxh7 Kf7 19.Be2 Qg5 20.Bc1! Bxh2+** (desperation, but 20...Qe5 21.Bh5+ Kf8 22.Qh8+ Ke7 23.Qxg7 is mate) **21.Kxh2! Qe5+ 22.f4! resigns** (22...Qxa1 23.Bh5+ or 22...Qxe2 23.Rxd8 is hopeless in either case).

part three
mastery

As you progress at chess, you find that it appears at times rather simple and at other times extraordinarily difficult. The moments when you think it is easy, however, are when you least understand the game. When you learn the game, the board is a vast sea of pieces all coming at you from unexpected directions. Gradually you learn to control the tactics, you acquire a quick sight of the board, and you learn to eliminate blunders. Well almost eliminate them, anyway. Your opponents continue blundering, and you win games by taking their pieces. It's all so easy.

As you meet stronger opponents, however, you start losing games without knowing where you're going wrong. Gradually you learn the rules of positional play. You stop creating unforced weaknesses in your position and you believe you have found the secret of invincibility. Then you move to a higher level and start losing all over again. And so it goes on. You can move to a deeper level of understanding only when you realize that there are vast areas of the game that elude your mental grasp.

The philosopher Noam Chomsky once mentioned chess as an example of something that is just beyond human mental abilities, but not so far beyond them that we cannot make a decent stab at it. We're very good at language, no better than rats at mazes, and somewhere in between at chess.

So how good is a chess master? A master, if the term is to mean anything, should be someone with at least a minimum level of professional competence. It's a player with enough technique to play fluent chess without thinking. It has been said that weak players think harder than strong ones. That's probably true. There are more things for them to work out. A strong player will smell out the potentially good moves and eliminate the bad without having to analyse them.

In this final section, we shall explore some of the themes that together comprise a master player's judgement. These can only come into play when your basic tactical and strategic skills have been formed. For these ideas are the fine-tuning of good chess. Some of them, you will discover, are aspects of the game that extend beyond the merely technical into the psychological nature of the chess struggle. The higher level you reach, the more important that becomes. Even if you never become a master player yourself, these ideas should help you appreciate and enjoy the games of the great players of the past, present and future.

5 the grand plan

We have spoken before of the importance of planning, and the non-existence of plans. It's time to explain what planning in chess really comprises. A strategic plan is not, as it is often portrayed, a clear path from the current position to victory, it is more like a vast flow-chart, with many decision points but each one containing an arrow leading you in the right direction.

For example: you move a piece into your opponent's half of the board; if he doesn't chase it away, it creates the cramped conditions that allow you to increase your control of space; if he chases it with pawns, they leave weak squares behind them; you manoeuvre a knight to occupy the weak squares; if he takes the knight, you recapture with a pawn to gain an endgame advantage; if he leaves the knight there, it forms the basis for an attack on his king; and so on, and so on.

At the end, you may join all the elements together and it shines through like a motorway on a road map. When you started, however, the whole plan was just a ragged lattice of interconnecting dark alleys.

> **Perfect strategies can only be seen with hindsight.**

Sometimes, of course, you will formulate an attacking idea that reaps dividends because your opponent did not see it coming: a little regroup-then-smite manoeuvre that catches him napping. It will feel like a strategic masterpiece when it comes off, but such a plan is little more than a commando raid. For total warfare, the Grand Plan leads from the opening through various possible middlegames into a number of different endgames. And whichever route the game takes, the Grand Plan is the logic that holds it all together.

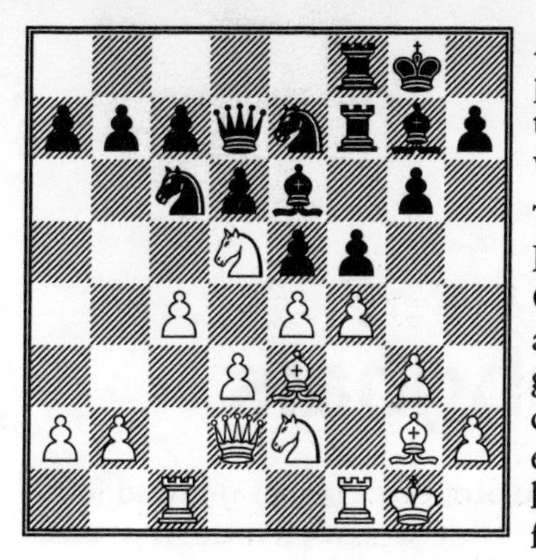

A level position with all the pieces still on the board. Black to play and plot a great victory.

The position comes from Benko–Botvinnik, Monte Carlo 1968. In his annotations written after the game, the former world champion, playing Black, explained the five stages of his winning strategy as follows.

(1) Exchange pawns immediately on e4 in order to ensure that White recaptures with the pawn rather than the bishop (since 1...fxe4 2.Bxe4 Nf5 favours Black). (2) Exchange white-squared bishops with Bh3, to eliminate a defender of e4. (3) Play exf4, forcing the recapture with the g-pawn. (4) Attack the e-pawn with Re8. (5) Meet Ng3 (defending the pawn) with h5 and h4, when the weakness of the e-pawn and white king must prove decisive.

The game continued **1...fxe4 2.dxe4 Nc8 3.c5 Bh3 4.b4 Bxg2 5.Kxg2 exf4 6.gxf4 Re8 7.Ng3 h5** and White's game was beginning to look ragged. Black won in another 15 moves. And if White had played 2.Bxe4, or 4.cxd6, or 6.Bxf4, or 7.Nbc3 instead of the moves in the game? Well then, of course, Black would have followed a totally different plan and written an equally lucid, but totally different note to the position in the diagram.

A great strategist such as Botvinnik has all the plans at his fingertips. The opponent, by his choice of moves, determines which one is used.

subgoals

While the concept of a Grand Strategic Plan, as outlined in the previous section, may be difficult to grasp, there is a much easier way of looking at it. Black's plan from the previous diagram position, seen as it unravelled rather than from the perspective of hindsight, was not so much a grand strategy as a series of subgoals. Botvinnik did not create a weakness in his opponent's position then exploit it; he first created a *potential* weakness, then turned it into a minor liability, then reduced White's mobility, then increased his space on the K-side. Even after all that, he did not have a winning position, perhaps not even a demonstrable advantage, but he was beginning to apply the strains to White's position that would bring about the decisive errors.

Wilhelm Steinitz, the first official world champion, was the first to enunciate the concept that games may be won by such a process of attrition rather than brilliant attacks. In 1885, he wrote this in the first volume of his *International Chess Magazine*:

'The indiscriminate and chiefly tactical king's side attack has been superseded by strategical manoeuvres, marches and counter-marches for gaining and accumulating small advantages at any point of the board, and the calculations and combinations are made subservient to the delicate shades of difference in the application of position judgment, like the melody is melted into the harmony and dramatic expression of Richard Wagner's music.'

In other words:

> **If you hoard your small advantages, the winning combinations will take care of themselves.**

While you must always stay alert for the chance of an effective piece of tactics, you do not need to worry where the brilliant finish is going to come from. If you steadily improve your position, the combinations arise naturally.

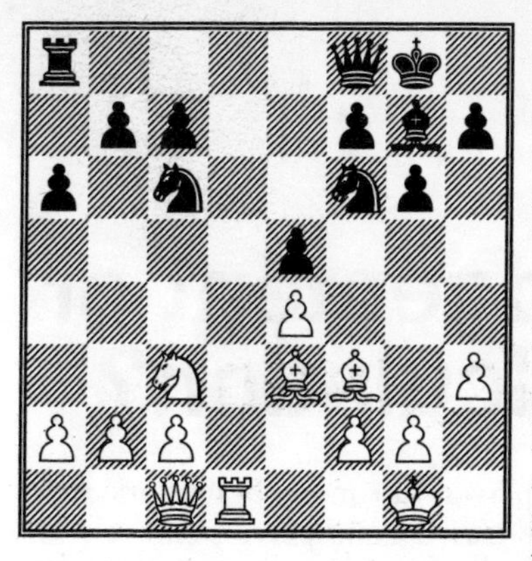

When the last round of the Keres Memorial Tournament in Tallinn 1979 began, Tigran Petrosian was half a point ahead of the field. Playing White against Gyula Sax, he seemed to be waiting to see how his rivals for first place, Tal and Vaganyan, were doing before compromising his own position in an attempt to win. This was the moment when he decided that he needed to win to stay ahead of Vaganyan. But how does White win such a sterile position? Answer: by accumulating small advantages.

Subgoal one Deny the d4 square to Black's knight: **1.Nb1! Rd8 2.Rxd8 Qxd8 3.c3! Qd3.**

Subgoal two Drive away that irritating queen: **4.Nd2 Bf8 5.Qb1! Qb5** (after 5...Qxb1+ 6.Nxb1, White plays to create Q-side weaknesses with moves such as b4, Nd2, Nb3, a4 and a later a5 or b5, or even Be2 and Bc4.) **6.Qc2 Nd8 7.Qb3 Qd3 8.Qc4 Qd6 9.Qe2 Qe6 10.Qd3 Bc6.**

Subgoal three Advance on the Q-side to create a weakness in Black's pawn formation: **11.a3 Qe7 12.b4 Nd8 13.Nc4 Nd7 14.Bg4 Ne6 15.Na5! b5 16.Nc6 Qe8.**

Subgoal four Expose the weakness: **17.c4!** and Black is already lost. After 17...bxc4 18.Qxc4, he cannot defend a6. Sax played **17...Nf6 18.cxb5 axb5 19.Qxb5 Nxe4** but after **20.Qc4 Nd6 21.Qd5** his game was almost hopeless. There followed **21...h5 22.Bxe6 fxe6 23.Qc5 Nf5 24.Qc2 Bg7 25.b5 Nd4 26.Qc4 Qd7 27.a4 Nf5 28.Qe2** and Black resigned. The a-pawn is too strong.

53 judgement or calculation?

It has been said that weak players do more brainwork than strong ones. That is probably true. Strong players can rely far more on judgement to tell them what moves are worth considering. A strong player may reject instinctively a move that a weaker one will have to analyse in depth. But how much should one trust one's judgement? When you feel that a move is wrong, but you cannot quite find the moves to prove it, do you let judgement overrule calculation or vice versa?

There is no clear answer to that question unless it is to say that judgement and calculation must be allowed to argue things over until they are reconciled. It is, after all, the counter-intuitive moves that make for great chess. But if judgement must always be supported by analysis, what's the point of making the judgements in the first place?

That's an easier one to answer.

> Chess is full of problems. You need good judgement to know if they have solutions.

You will not find a winning combination without first sensing that one is in the air. You will not find the right path to equality unless you correctly judge that such a path is there in the first place.

Players make concessions and accept weaknesses unnecessarily because their judgement is at fault. They miss clear winning opportunities because their judgement does not tell them to search for them. Looking for a good chess move is like looking for a lost sock: the search becomes far more directed and systematic if you have good reason to believe that what you are looking for is there to be found.

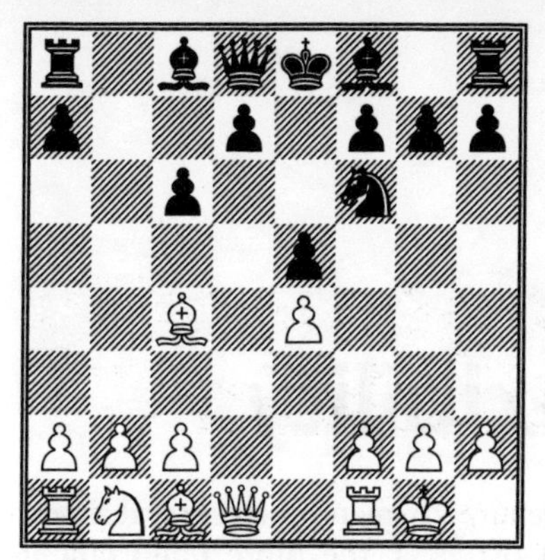

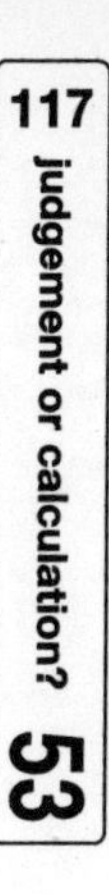

Black to play. Should he take the pawn on e4, or not?

Wilhelm Steinitz quoted this position from a Morphy–Lowenthal game as an example of the superiority of the 'modern' (Steinitzian) judgemental school over the older (Morphy) calculation-based play. Lowenthal played 1...d5, which led him into difficulties by opening the game with his king still in the centre. Steinitz claimed that Black should take on e4 without thinking: 'Any first-class player would grasp at it now without wasting much of his time allowance, and probably a second rate man, who has followed the notes of modern analysts, would not hesitate much.'

Judgement told Steinitz that it must be good, on principle, to take an opponent's centre pawn. What is interesting, however, is the way he then produces analysis to substantiate his claim. Lowenthal claimed that 1...Nxe4 was too dangerous, citing the variation 2.Re1 d5 3.Rxe4! when 3...dxe4 loses the queen to 4.Bxf7+!

Steinitz, however, with the conviction that 1...Nxe4 must be correct, paused to look more deeply at the position after 3.Rxe4 and found the reply 3...f6! Now the threat of dxe4 is real and Black must regain his piece with advantage. 4.Rxe5+ fxe5 5.Qh5+ Kd7 is insufficient for White and the sly 4.b3!? hoping for 4...dxe4 5.Bf7+ Ke7 6.Ba3+ is calmly met by 4...Be7!

Lowenthal and Morphy were both seduced by pretty tactics with 3.Rxe4 dxe4 4.Bxf7+. Steinitz started with the assumption that 1...Nxe4 must be the correct move, so forced himself to find out what was wrong with White's idea.

54 flexibility

'Flexibility' is a word we have already mentioned several times, and the higher the standard of chess, the more important it becomes. A good game of chess is like a long baseline rally in tennis. Each player endeavours to manoeuvre the other one until he is sufficiently out of place to allow a winning shot in an area of the board/court that he cannot reach. Any chess position is in a constant state of dynamism, with a variety of attacks and manoeuvres lurking in the realms of strategic possibility, but waiting for the most auspicious moment. The key to maintaining the correct balance is flexibility.

When direct attacks do not achieve anything, one must look for a move that will come in useful whatever direction the game turns. It may be a move that seems to accomplish nothing immediately, but will surely come in useful later – if only to deter the opponent from an otherwise promising continuation.

> The most difficult moves to find are the ones that do nothing.

Especially when the position holds a good deal of tension, the temptation to do something can be very strong, but the true art of fine positional play is to maintain flexibility, holding the tension until it can be released with the maximum effect – or until one's opponent is forced to release it himself in unfavourable circumstances.

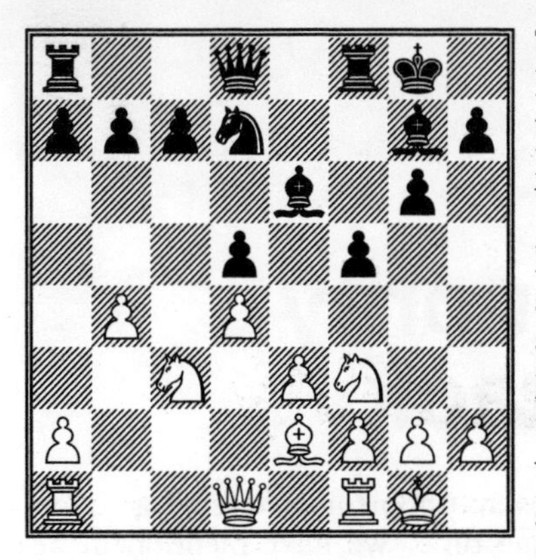

This was the position after Black's 12th move, 12...f5, in the game Karpov–Korchnoi, London 1984. What should White play now?

Black's last move signals his aggressive intentions: he may, according to circumstances, play ...f4, or ...g5 and g4, or ...Nf6 and Ne4.

White's most natural moves appear to be 13.Qb3 (attacking d5 and supporting the b-pawn) or 13.Rb1 (to help a later push of the b-pawn) or 13.Rc1 to begin operations on the c-file. Instead Karpov played the hyper-flexible (though at first sight irrelevant) **13.Re1!**

Far from being pointless, however, the move is full of latent strength.

- The rook is beautifully placed to meet a later ...f4 either with exf4, when it will pose immediate threats on the e-file, or perhaps even with e4 again opening the e-file to give the rook activity.
- If Black plays ...Nf6 and Ne4, White may want to expel it by moving the knight from f3, then playing f3. In that case the rook stands best on e1, both to defend e3 and to prepare a later break with e4.
- Meanwhile, on the Q-side, the most likely change in structure is for Black to play ...c6 and meet b5 with ...c5. White's dxc5 will then leave Black with an isolated d-pawn, which he will want to exchange by advancing it to d4 – when again the rook on e1 will then come into action after exd4.
- Finally, if Black is going to attack on the K-side, it might be wise to keep the queen on d1 rather than stray off to b3 right now.

This may all seem far-fetched, but look how the game continued: **13...g5 14.Rc1 Kh8 15.Bd3 c6 16.b5 g4 17.Nd2 c5 18.dxc5 Nxc5 19.Nb3 Nxb3 20.axb3** and just when Black wanted to play ...d4, he was unable to do so because of the rook on e1. After 20...Rc8 21.Ne2 Rxc1 22.Qxc1 Qb6 23.Nf4 White held the advantage and went on to win in 38 moves.

55 minority attack

The previous diagram gives us an opportunity to enlarge upon two recent themes at the same time. We have mentioned the idea of a Grand Plan and we have just spoken of Flexibility. The Minority Attack gives a specific example of both ideas.

Under most circumstances, you need a preponderance of pieces in a particular area of the board to expect an attack to be successful. But here's the paradox:

> **A minority of pawns on one wing can be used to create structural damage in the opponent's camp.**

The typical position arises when both sides have pushed their d-pawns two squares forwards, Black has met White's c4 advance with e6, and cxd5 has been answered by exd5. White then has a minority of pawns on the Q-side and the Minority Attack is ready to swing into operation. It gives a fine example of the sort of flow-chart referred to in Section 51.

Black plays c6, White plays b4. Black may then allow b5, or prevent it by playing b5 himself. If Black plays ...b5, he will try to bring a knight quickly to c4, to shield the c-pawn. White may aim to bring his own knight to c5, or aim for a break in the centre with e4. If Black does not play ...b5, White will advance b5 himself which Black may meet by: a) allowing bxc6 and meeting it with bxc6; b) allowing bxc6 and recapturing with a piece on c6; c) playing cxb5 himself; or d) playing c5. The first of these leaves him with a backward c-pawn, the others all leave an isolated d-pawn.

In a nutshell, that's the Minority Attack, and we have not even touched upon the other branches of the flow-chart where Black pre-empts b4 by playing ...a5, or where White shifts his attention to the centre and plays for f3 and e4.

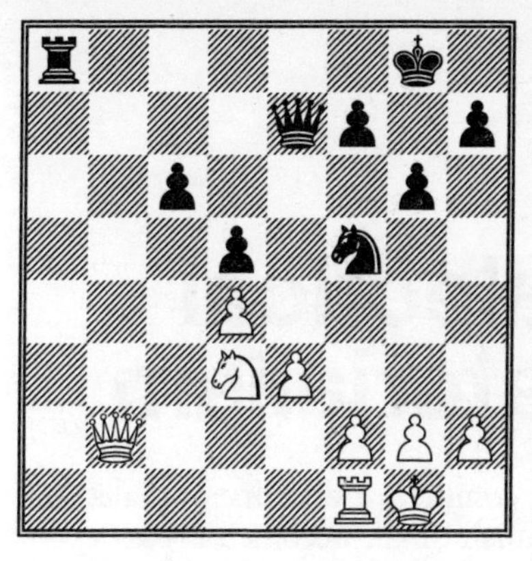

Reaping the rewards. This position, from Byrne–Eliskases, Helsinki 1952, was the typical result of a successful Minority Attack. White's b4 had been met by ...a6; he continued with a4 and b5, when ...axb5 eliminated the a-pawns and bxc6 led to the structure now on the board. Black's only weakness is the pawn on c6, which can be defended as easily as it can be attacked, but this still formed the basis for White's victory.

There followed: **1.Rc1 Nh4** (tricky: he plans to meet Rxc6 with Nxg2! and Qe4+) **2.Qe2 Ra3** (with the same idea) **3.g3 Qe4 4.Ne1 Nf5** (now the plan is 5.Rxc6 Nxe3!) **5.Qc2! Qxc2 6.Rxc2 Ne7 7.Kf1 f6 8.Ke2 Kf7 9.Nd3 Ke6 10.Rb2 Ra7 11.g4!** (White cannot win solely by pressure against c6; he must create an object of attack on the K-side too.) **11...g5 12.Rb8 Kf7 13.Rh8 Kg7 14.Rd8 Rc7 15.Nc5 Kf7 16.Kf3 Ng6 17.Kg3 Ra7 18.Rd6 Rc7** (18...Ne7 would have been strongly met by 19.Nd7.) **19.Na6 Rc8 20.Rd7+ Ne7 21.Nc5 Ra8 22.Rd6 Ra1** (This hastens the end, but Black was unwilling to remain totally passive. After 22...Rc8, White can increase the pressure with h4 followed by f3 and e4.) **23.Nd7 f5 24.Ne5+ Kg7 25.h3!** (calmly does it) **25...fxg4 26.fxg4 Rc1 27.Re6! Ng6** (27...Kf8 loses a pawn to the simple 28.Nf3) **28.Rxc6** and White's extra pawn was enough to win the game.

White's play in this sequence was the classical strategy: use one enemy weakness to tie your opponent down, then stretch his defences by attacking something on the other wing. His task would have been made far more difficult had Black seen it all coming and played ...h5! somewhere between moves 7 and 10.

56 dialectical materialism

A fundamental precept of the communist doctrine of dialectical materialism was that capitalism had become a barrier to progress. Much the same can be true on a chessboard, though the materialist inclination always exerts a powerful influence on our thought processes. The temptation to cash in a positional advantage for a concrete gain in material is strong, but bear this in mind:

> An enemy pawn in the hand may be worth less than one on the board.

Capturing a pawn may free the opponent in two ways. Firstly, and most obviously, it will free the pieces that would otherwise have had to defend that pawn. Secondly, it may open important lines and free for later use the square on which that pawn stood.

There is another side to this concept too: sometimes it is better for a defender to surrender a pawn rather than stubbornly keep it defended. Imagine the following endgame: each side has a rook and four pawns; white has four pawns on the K-side and a rook on a6; Black has three K-side pawns, a pawn on a7 and a rook on c7; both kings are behind their K-side pawns. I have several times seen players lose the black side of such endgames by refusing to give up the a-pawn. While White advances his pawns and his king, eventually creating fatal weaknesses, Black just sits there, locked behind his third rank by the white rook. Instead, he should, at some stage, give up the pawn, when the endgame is usually a draw. But throwing a pawn overboard is something most players find difficult to do.

Black to play: what result?

White to play: what result?

This position, from Pachman–Hromadka, Prague 1944, is a remarkably instructive example of the way capitalism may impede progress.

Objectively, it should not matter whose move it is: Black's bishop is bad enough to lose the game for him. For example, with Black to move, the game might continue 1...Bd4 2.Ne1 Bf2 3.Nf3 Bd4 4.Nh4+ Kf6 5.Kh5 Bf2 6.Nf5 Bg1 7.Nh6 Bd4 8.Ng4+ Ke6 9.Kg6 Bg1 10.Nh6 Bd4 11.Nf7 Be3 12.Ng5+ Kd6 (12...Bxg5 13.Kxg5 is hopeless for Black) 13.Kf5 Bd4 14.Nf7+ Ke7 15.Nxe5. White then has various ways to win, including the simple plan of Nd3, e5, Ke4, Nf4 (if necessary to chase the black king from e6), Kd5 and Nd3 winning the c-pawn too.

In fact, it was White's move in the actual game and, instead of following the same plan with 1.Ne1 he made the greedy error of 1.Nxc5? after which the position is probably drawn! Black plays 1...Kf6 and brings his king as rapidly as possible to d6 or c6. The threat of winning the c-pawn makes it impossible for White to continue with his winning plan. For example 2.Nd3 Ke6 3.c5 Kd7 4.Kf5 Kc6 when 5.Nxe5+ Kxc5 leaves a drawn endgame, while 5.Ke6 Bc3 leaves White unable to make progress. White's best chance is to bring his king over to the Q-side beginning with 2.Kf3, and leaving the pawn on c4, but Black can probably still hold the draw. Even if White can win, the materialistic 1.Nxc5 is certainly a more difficult way to do so than the purely technical plan outlined above. Black's position oddly improves once the pawn disappears from c5. With that square available for his king, Black has far better defensive possibilities.

25 material and time

In the previous section, we saw it may be a poor decision, on positional grounds, to win one of your opponent's pawns. Even though any win of material is tempting, it ought not to be difficult to see the advantages of leaving your opponent with a pawn that is interfering with the communications between his own pieces. Even more difficult, however, is to take the decision not to capture a pawn because it slows down a positional plan.

The great 18th-century French champion François André Danican-Philidor assessed the value of a pawn to be three moves in development. Since the capture of any pawn is liable to cost two moves (one to take it and one to return to base), that means you should think twice about making any pawn-capturing detour. Philidor's rate of exchange, however, was designed for play in the openings. In the middle game, such valuations become more fluid. In some positions, time is of the essence and a pawn or two may be irrelevant to the main business. In others, the win of any pawn is a matter for great celebration.

A pawn is a pawn, but two moves may be more useful.

When you have built up a favourable position and have the chance to win a pawn, usually it will be the right thing to do, but it is always worth sparing a thought to ask whether the time you spend capturing it will give your opponent the chance to get back into the game.

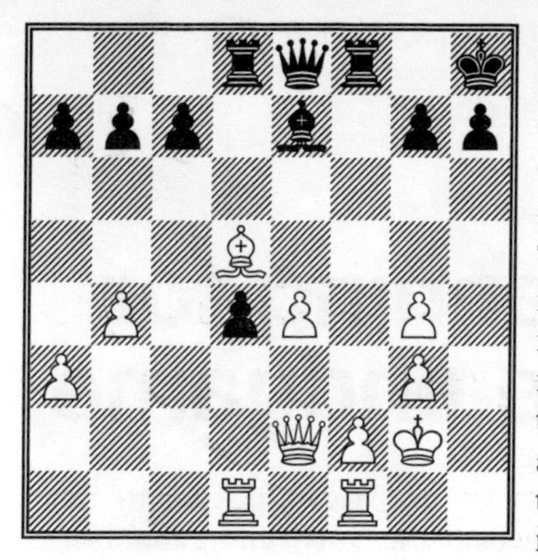

White to play. Should he pocket the pawn on b7 or not?

The position arose in the third game of the Botvinnik–Tal World Championship match in 1961. White has a number of advantages: the mobile mass of K-side pawns; the chance of mounting an attack down the h-file and on the white squares; the possibility of taking the pawn on b7.

The average strong player will think: 'I've outplayed him so far, now is the time to cash in the benefits,' and will play 1.Bxb7.

A more cautious player might see the variation 1.Bxb7 d3!? 2.Rxd3 Qb5 and be frightened off.

A less jumpy individual might decide that 1.Bxb7 d3 2.Qe3 is rather good for White after all.

But it took a great player like Botvinnik to ignore the pawn on b7 totally and play **1.Bc4!** White plans to continue with Rh1, Bd3, f4 and e5, with an irresistible attack. The game continued **1...c5 2.b5 Bf6 3.f4 d3** (a desperate attempt to exchange pieces and gain a little room to manoeuvre before he is squashed by e5 and Bd3) **4.Rxd3 Rxd3 5.Bxd3 Bd4 6.e5 g6 7.Rh1 Kg7 8.Qe4 b6 9.Bc4.** Here the game was adjourned, but **Black resigned** without resuming play. After 9...Qe7 (as good as anything) 10.g5 White threatens Qc6 followed by Qf6+, and 10...Rc8 is dealt with by means of 11.f5! gxf5 12.Rxh7+! Kxh7 13.Qh4+ and 14.Qh6 mate.

While Black's resignation seems a little premature, it is clear there is nothing he can do against a systematic advance of White's e- and f-pawns.

58 planning for the endgame

While we are on the subject of not accepting pawns from strange men, there is one more example worth citing that brings in another important theme. However deeply engrossed you may be in the intricacies of the middlegame, you should always be thinking, at least in the back of your mind, about the endgames that may result from exchanges.

The transition from middlegame to ending is one of the most vital aspects of strategic play. When you lose a game without knowing where you went wrong, the chances are that it was in this phase of the game. Indeed, even in the opening, it pays to keep half an eye on the various endgame possibilities.

You should always be asking yourself which pieces you would like to retain in an endgame and which would benefit you to be exchanged. If you have an advantage, how can you realize your strategic objectives without giving your opponent the chance to bale out into a tenable endgame? If you are grimly defending, how can you salvage half a point by swapping off the right places?

> In the transition from middlegame to endgame, large advantages can turn into draws and small disadvantages may become losses.

As we have seen before, the inherent uncertainty of middlegame evaluations dissolves into a far clearer picture when the endgame is reached. Switching from one to another demands considerable flexibility in one's thinking patterns if the correct decisions are to be reached.

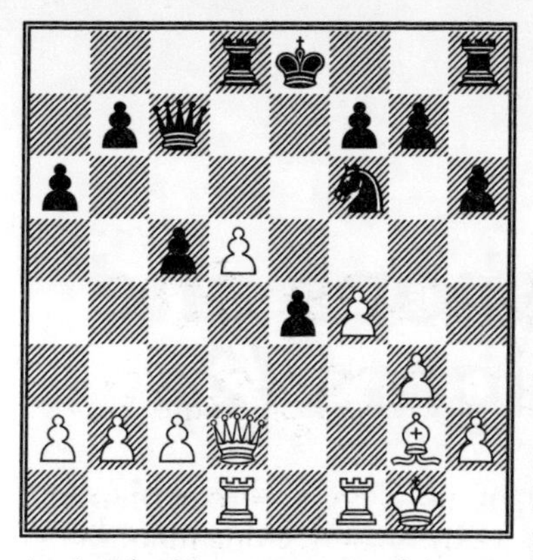

White to play in Fischer–Taimanov, Vancouver 1971. What should he do about the attack on his d-pawn? Push it with 1.d6; defend it with 1.c4; or do you have an even better idea?

Having eliminated 1.d6, on the grounds that after 1...Qc6 or Qb6 the pawn on d6 is more likely to be a liability than a strength, most players would quickly opt for 1.c4. Black's pawn on e4 is not going to be easy to defend if White doubles rooks on the e-file and supports the attack with Qc2. So let's play c4, round up the e-pawn, then think again.

Fischer, however, pursued that thought and came to a very different conclusion. Just suppose White does play c4 then attack e4 with everything he owns. Black will probably double rooks on the e-file too, then after Bxe4 he will wait for the bishop to move, then exchange all the rooks. Finally, Black will position his knight on d6 and challenge White to make progress. White's bishop has nothing to do and, despite his extra pawn, the game will probably end in a draw.

Instead Fischer continued **1.Rfe1! Rxd5 2.Rxe4+ Kd8 3.Qe2 Rxd1+ 4. Qxd1+ Qd7 5.Qxd7+ Kxd7 6.Re5 b6 7.Bf1 a5 8.Bc4 Rf8** and won a long and beautiful endgame in which his rook and bishop proved themselves superior to the black rook and knight. (See the next section for full details.)

In effect, the decision Fischer took in the diagram position was to prefer a position with level material but a clear and permanent positional advantage to one in which he would have been a pawn ahead but with little prospect of making that advantage felt. Even when expressed as plausibly as this, however, such a decision can be difficult to make.

59 bishops and knights (2)

First they tell you that knights are better than bishops in blocked positions. Then they tell you that bishops are better than knights when there is play on both sides of the board. Then they say that knights are better than bishops when the pawn structure is symmetrical – because passed pawns will then not feature to shift attention from wing to wing. Finally they tell you that bishops are better than knights when the bishop can find something to attack.

It's all very confusing. The nearest one can get to a definitive evaluation combines elements of all these rules of thumb.

> A bishop is better than a knight when widely separated areas of the board demand attention simultaneously, and the bishop is able to affect play in both areas at the same time.

When the pawn structure is still fluid, the player with a bishop against a knight should strive to obtain just such a position. As long as attention is liable to shift rapidly from side to side, the bishop is likely to be the superior piece – as long as it can actually find something to do, or at least help the pieces that can affect matters directly.

One word of caution, however: positions in which a knight is superior to a bishop tend to be easier to play for the side with the advantage than positions in which a bishop is better than a knight. One slip with a good knight against a bad bishop is liable to make little difference – the plodding knight can just work its way round again to re-create the opportunity. But a mistake with the bishop may allow a knight in to gobble up some defenceless pawns. A good bishop, after all, tends to be one that is not defending its own pawns.

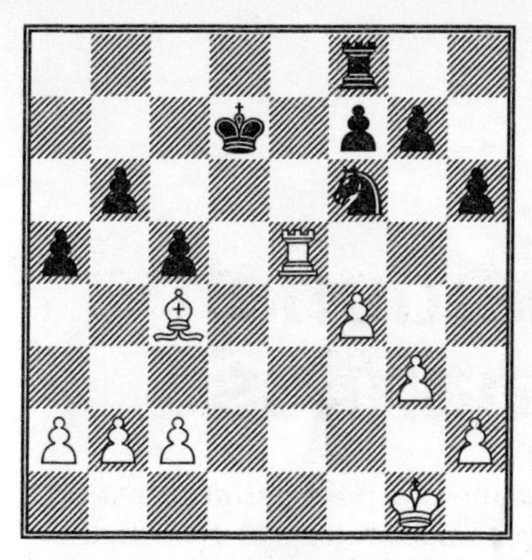

Here is the position in which we left Fischer and Taimanov last time. Black's rook has just moved to defend the f-pawn. How is White to create the conditions that make his bishop decisively superior to the knight?

As usual, the key must be to create points of attack on both wings. The Q-side is already catered for: White's long-term objective is to infiltrate with his king to b5. This alone, however, cannot be enough; White must also fix the K-side pawns in a manner that gives him hopes of infiltration on that wing too.

The game continued **1.Kg2 Kd6 2.Kf3 Nd7. 3.Re3 Nb8 4.Rd3+ Kc7 5.c3 Nc6 6.Re3 Kd6 7.a4 Ne7 8.h3 Nc6 9.h4 h5** (Worried about White's plan of h5, g4, g5, Kg4 and gxh6 followed by Kf5 and Kf6, Taimanov puts a stop to the pawn advance.) **10.Rd3+ Kc7 11.Rd5 f5 12.Rd2 Rf6 13.Re2 Kd7 14.Re3 g6 15.Bb5 Rd6 16.Ke2 Kd8 17.Rd3! Kc7 18.Rxd6 Kxd6 19.Kd3 Ne7** (Both sides have been aiming for this position. With a blocked pawn formation and no passed pawns on the horizon, Black trusted his knight, but Fischer had judged it better.) **20.Be8!** (tying the knight to defence of g6) **20...Kd5 21.Bf7+ Kd6 22.Kc4 Kc6 23.Be8+ Kb7 24.Kb5 Nc8 25.Bc6+** (not 25.Bxg6?? Nd6 mate) **25...Kc7 26.Bd5 Ne7 27.Bf7 Kb7 28.Bb3! Ka7 29.Bd1 Kb7 30.Bf3+ Kc7** (30...Ka7 31.Bg2 Ng8 32.Kc6 Nf6 33.Kd6 Ne4+ 34.Ke6 Nxg3 35.Kf6 Ne2 36.Kg5! leads to a win for White.) **31.Ka6! Ng8 32.Bd5 Ne7 33.Bc4! Nc6 34.Bf7 Ne7 35.Be8! Kd8** (the only move) **36.Bxg6! Nxg6 37.Kxb6 Kd7 38.Kxc5** and the lumbering knight was no match for the white pawns: **38...Ne7 39.b4 axb4 40.cxb4 Nc8 41.a5 Nd6 42.b5 Ne4+ 43.Kb6 Kc8 44.Kc6! Kb8 45.b6 resigns.**

09 positional dynamics

Most advice you will see on evaluating positions deals with the problem by considering tactics and strategy as two separate entities. You make a dynamic evaluation of the tactical possibilities by calculating all forcing variations, and you make a static evaluation of the strategic possibilities. At the end of each tactical variation, you add up the material on the two sides, you compare the weaknesses, and you look at the relative effectiveness of Black's and White's positions.

There is, however, another level of strategic judgement in which it is insufficient to look at the static features of a position. For certain features of a position, however much they may form part of the landscape, are liable to change. Those potential changes form the strategic dynamics of a position, which is the most difficult aspect of positional assessment to come to terms with.

> It is not enough to consider only the structural features of a position; one must also take into account what they are liable to turn into in the future.

We have met one example of this idea already. In the Minority Attack, Black has a perfectly sound structure with pawns on a7, b7, c6 and d5 free from weaknesses. As we have seen, however, if White plays b4 and b5, Black cannot avoid a weakness being created.

You may apply all the rules of sound strategy to a position and emerge with a clean bill of health. Yet a few moves later, you will find yourself with weaknesses, and there was no way to avoid them. Statically, your position was sound, but the strategic dynamics were against you.

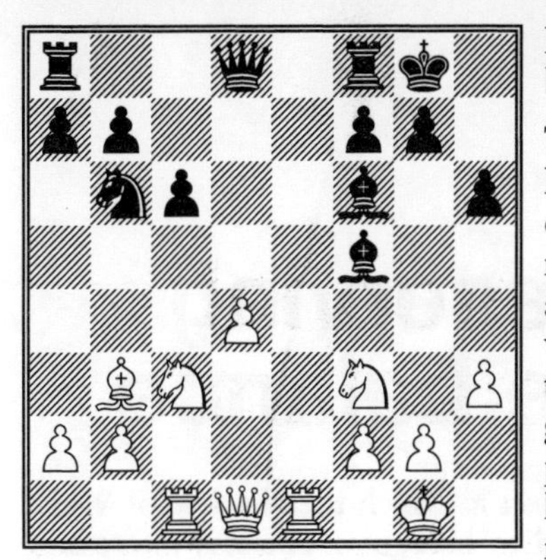

Black to play. Who stands better?

The world champion, Garry Kasparov, made a good living out of this position in the mid-1980s. Any static assessment of the position would be bound to conclude that Black has a perfectly good game: he has the bishop pair in an open position; all his pieces are active; he has no weaknesses and the white d-pawn is isolated.

Black's latent drawbacks only emerge when you begin to consider the ways in which the position may metamorphose. White plans to increase the pressure on the b3–f7 diagonal by playing Ne5. If Black captures the knight with his bishop when it reaches e5, then he is left with a bishop distinctly more passive than White's. If he anticipates Ne5 by playing ...Nd7, then White may consider playing d5, liquidating his isolated pawn and leaving himself with pressure against both f7 and b7. If he plays ...Nd5, then Nxd5 followed by Ne5 will favour White. Black's position is fine as it stands, but White has far greater potential for improvement.

Kasparov–Short, Brussels 1986, gave a drastic example of the way play can develop: **1...Bg5** (expecting 2.Nxg5 Qxg5) **2.Ra1! Nd7 3.d5! Rc8 4.Nd4 Bg6 5.Ne6! fxe6 6.dxe6 Kh7 7.Qxd7 Qb6 8.e7 Rfe8** (White cannot maintain his pawn on e7, but while Black is winning it he conjures up a winning attack.) **9.Qg4! Qc5 10.Ne4! Qxe7 11.Bc2! Rf8 12.g3! Qd8** (the threat was 13.f4) **13.Rad1 Qa5 14.h4! Be7 15.Nc3! Bxc2 16.Rxe7 Rg8 17.Rdd7 Bf5 18.Rxg7+ Kh8 19.Qd4 resigns.**

9 preserving the balance

There are two types of position in which the chances of White and Black may fairly be said to be equal. The less interesting type is where nothing much is happening. The two armies may have met in the centre and led to a blocked position, or they may be quietly getting on with their own manoeuvres, hardly having come into contact with one another. In any case there are no imminent skirmishes and the real battles have either already been fought or are well over the horizon.

Then there are the exciting positions of dynamic equilibrium where chances are balanced because threats, counter-threats and mutual defences, both actual and potential, hold each other at bay in a state of heightened tension. In such positions the task of each player is to preserve the balance.

> In positions of dynamic equilibrium, the player who first upsets the balance is the one who loses.

Like a boxer who lets down his guard momentarily when trying to throw an unjustified punch – and gets walloped for his error – a good player must keep his nerve, and his defences, intact and not upset the balance.

It often all comes back to a feeling for the centre of gravity of a position. A complex position can be like a cumbersome object resting on a small base. If you move one piece to the wrong square, it moves the centre of gravity and causes the whole thing to topple over.

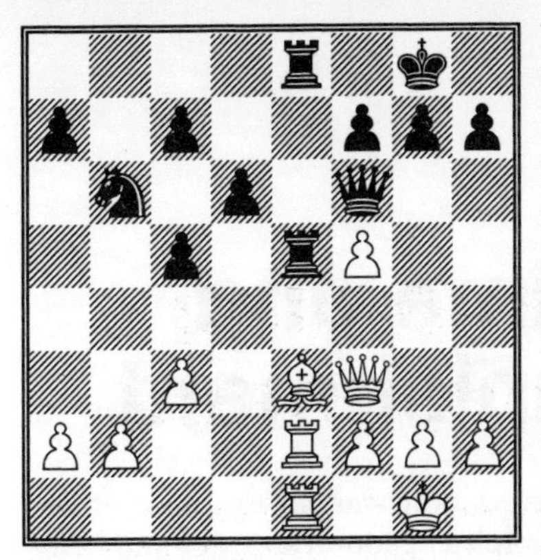

White to play, in Alekhine–Capablanca, St Petersburg 1914. All the action centres on the e-file and f5-square. How can White preserve the balance?

Perhaps the first thing to note is there is no real threat to the f-pawn. If it were Black's move, 1...Rxf5 could be met by 2.Bg5! or 1...Qxf5 by 2.Qxf5 Rxf5 3.Bxc5! Nevertheless, the defence of f5 will surely soon be a pressing problem. White might consider 1.Bd2 or 1.Bc1, attempting to exchange some rooks, or 1.g4, supporting f5.

Instead, the young Alekhine, playing his first game against the man he was to defeat 13 years later for the world championship, upset the balance with **1.Qb7?**

On tactical grounds, the move looks justifiable as it gets the queen in among the black Q-side pawns, but there is too much happening on the other wing – where, after all, White's king resides – for such a policy to be justifiable. There followed **1...Qxf5 2.Qxc7 Qe6 3.Qxa7 Nd5!** Now Black is beautifully centralized and there is no quick way for the white queen to return to the defence. The game continued **4.Kf1 Nf4! 5.Rd2 Nxg2! 6.Kxg2 Qg4+ 7.Kf1** (7.Kh1 Rg5! 8.Qb7 d5 loses at once for White) **7...Qh3+ 8.Ke2 Rxe3+!** (With this, Black regains his sacrificed piece and wins the game because of the exposed white king.) **9.fxe3 Qxe3+ 10.Kd1 Qxe1+ 11.Kc2 Qe4+ 12.Kb3 Qc6 13.a4 d5 14.a5 Qb5+ 15.Ka3 Rb8 16.Ka2 h6 17.a6 Qb3+ White resigned.** After 18.Kb1 Re8 19.Rc2 Re1+ 20.Rc1 Re2 it is all over.

Capablanca did not need to see any of this when he allowed 1.Qb7 in the diagram position. His positional sense would have told him that the move was wrong and, as usual, he found precisely the correct way to prove it.

62 crime and punishment

What we saw in the previous section was an example of one player sinning against the principles of sound strategy and being punished for it by simple, correct play. Sometimes, however, a crime may only be punished by a move, or series of moves, that appears to transgress the game's principles themselves. And this explains why one of the great paradoxes of chess is doubly true:

> You can win a game by playing bad moves.

Firstly, you can win a game by playing 'bad moves' – meaning moves that offend normal principles – as the correct means of exploiting a previous error of the opponent.

Secondly, you can win a game by making objectively bad moves, when your opponent cannot bring himself to make the necessary bad-looking moves in reply. When Alekhine played 1.Qb7 in the previous position, it might well have won the game for him against a lesser opponent. If Capablanca had meekly tried to defend his Q-side pawns instead of sacrificing them, it could have led to White's seizing the initiative. While we should not want to encourage the deliberate playing of bad moves, it can often be true that dubious moves set the opponent more problems than correct ones.

Again we come back to the relationship between judgement and calculation. You need good judgement to sense when your opponent has made a mistake. When that happens, you know you must look for a way to exploit it, and that (as long as your initial judgement was correct) gives you permission to break the normal rules of sound play yourself.

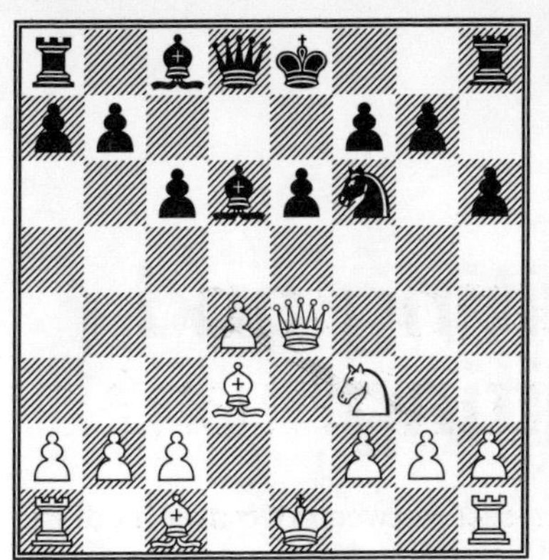

White to play in Kamsky–Karpov, Dortmund 1993. His queen is attacked, and White must decide whether to retreat it to e2 – not especially aggressive, but ready for action in the centre, K-side or Q-side when necessary – or commit the queen to the K-side with **1.Qh4** as Kamsky played. How should Black react?

The obvious developing move is 1...0-0, but this runs into great trouble against 2.Bxh6! gxh6 3.Qxh6 when the threat of 4.Ng5 gives White a winning attack.

Black can exchange the dangerous white queen with 1...Nd5 2.Qxd8+ Kxd8 or 1...Qa5+ 2.Bd2 Qh5 3.Qxh5 Nxh5, but either of those leaves him with an uninspiring position. Black could try 1...Be7, but it seems illogical to move the bishop again, especially to an inherently less active square.

Karpov's solution was astonishing and only explicable when seen as a way of punishing White for the decentralizing 1.Qh4. He played **1...Ke7!!** as a means of protecting his rook on h8 and thereby threatening 2...g5! Suddenly White's king does not look so well placed on h4 after all. White can play 2.Bf4, in order to meet 2...g5 with 3.Bxd6+ Qxd6 4.Qg3, when Black's position has been rather loosened by his pawn advance, but simply 2...Bb4+ 3.Bd2 (otherwise...g5 comes) 3...Bxd2+ leaves Black comfortably placed. He can always castle manually with ...Re8 (or Rd8) and Kf8 if need be.

Kamsky played **2.Ne5!?** sacrificing a pawn after **2...Bxe5 3.dxe5 Qa5+ 4.c3 Qxe5+.** With his king in the centre, Black needed to play cautiously after the further moves **5.Be3 b6 6.0-0-0 g5 7.Qa4 c5 8.Rhe1 Bd7,** but with an extra pawn, his position was preferable.

Had Black not found the extravagant 1...Ke7! White's Qh4 would have looked like a good move. In order to expose it as inferior to the more flexible 1.Qe2, Black had to break the rules himself.

63 writing and editing

Many novelists stress the difference between two aspects of the creative process. First comes the writing: the characters and plot are defined, the problems they face are identified and resolved, and by the time that is done, the first draft is ready. Then comes the editing stage, with its fine-tuning and polishing, when all the style is put into the work. For some writers, it is essential to separate these two stages. When the mind is in a creative phase, it is impossible to pay the close attention to detail that editing demands; and when it is engaged in editing, there is no hope of taking an overall view of the grand scheme of the work.

Chess players have the same problem: the vague thought processes of general planning are incompatible with the detailed analysis of tactics. In 'writing' mode, the player is looking for ideas, sensing possibilities, and improving his general feel of the position; in 'editing' mode, he analyses concrete variations.

The routine most players naturally fall into is to 'write' when it is the opponent's turn to move – gazing vaguely at the board, or even walking around the room, letting ideas gestate – and 'edit' when their own clocks are running. Which explains one important paradox:

> It is easy to blunder when your opponent is short of time.

When you have been jolted out of your 'writing' mode by a quick response, it is easy to make a huge misjudgement. One solution is to make a conscious break in your thoughts, just to switch from one mode to another. And that is why the old school of Soviet grandmasters in the 1950s and 1960s always wrote down their moves before playing them. Think, decide, write ... then ask yourself: 'Is this a blunder?' By breaking your thought patterns before asking the question, you are more likely to come up with the correct answer.

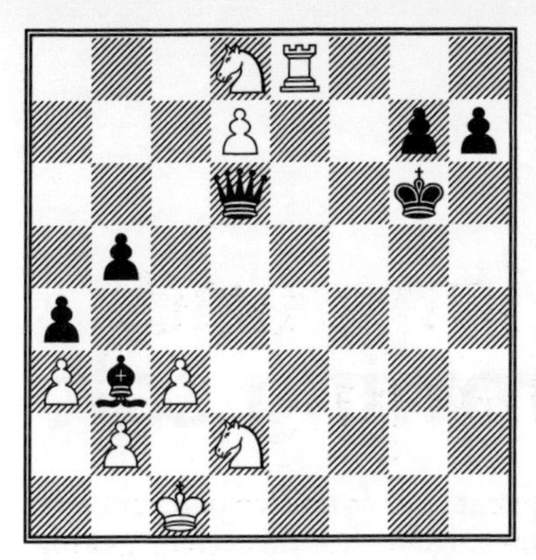

Pathology of a disaster. It is White to play in Short–Kasparov, 10th game, 1993 World Championship, and he must choose the most effective way to force his passed pawn home.

One good idea is 1.Re6+ Bxe6 2.Nxe6 Qxe6 (2...Qxd7 loses to 3.Nf8+) 3.d8=Q when White's extra piece should win the endgame.

Another good idea is **1.Ne6!** as Short played. Since 1...Bxe6 loses to 2.d8=Q and 1...Qxd7 loses to 2.Nf8+, Kasparov tried to confuse matters with **1...Qh2(!)**. There followed **2.Nf4+ Kh6 3.Nd3 Qg1+** when White suddenly noticed that the intended 4.Ne1 would be met by 4...Qg4!!, threatening both Qxd7 and Qd1 mate. The game therefore continued **4.Re1 Qg5 5.Ne5 g6 6.Rf1 Be6 7.Nf7+ Bxf7 8.Rxf7 Qd5 9.Re7 Qd6 10.Rf7 Qd3 11.Ne4 Qe3+ 12.Nd2 Qd3 draw agreed.**

Had White found time to draw breath in this sequence, and move into writing rather than editing mode, he would surely have spotted one of several winning chances.

- Instead of 2.Nf4+, he could have won at once with 2.Rf8!, meeting any queen check with 3.Rf1.
- Instead of 5.Ne5, he could have played 5.Rh1+ Kg6 6.Ne5+! Kf5 7.Nc6!
- And instead of 9.Re7?, he could have played 9.Ne4! Qd3 10.Rf2 Qxd7 11.Rh2+ Kg7 12.Rxh7+! Kxh7 13.Nf6+.

White simply let the tension of the occasion and some unexpected tactics throw his normal thinking patterns completely off balance.

throwing salt

Each bout of Sumo wrestling begins, before the contestants try to shove each other out of the ring, with a display of glaring, squatting, stamping on the ground and throwing copious handfuls of salt. It is all part of a ritual face-off during which the wrestlers size each other up and build up their concentration for the ensuing fight. It is said that some 70 per cent of all contests are decided during the face-off, before the wrestlers make physical contact. One man becomes so intimidated by his opponent's confidence, by his very presence in the ring, that he knows he will lose.

No wonder then that so many grandmasters are Sumo fans. For while every chess game is being fought out on the board, a similar face-off takes place between the players. And it lasts the entire duration of the game. From the initial handshake to final resignation, every gesture, every twitch, every change of body posture plays its part in each player's attempt to assert his authority. Few players indulge in deliberate gamesmanship, but even fewer fail to influence their opponents unwittingly through body language at some stage of the game.

Players frequently glance at each other's faces, not in any conscious attempt to read lips or minds, but because a lifetime's experience has taught them, whether they realize it or not, that valuable information is gleaned by doing so. The young Boris Spassky taught himself to adopt a perfectly blank expression – a 'clown's face', as he called it – to avoid giving his opponents information on his emotional reactions to their moves.

> Poker faces work at chess too.

Sensing what your opponent thinks about the position is a valuable asset; it pays not to let him know what you're thinking too.

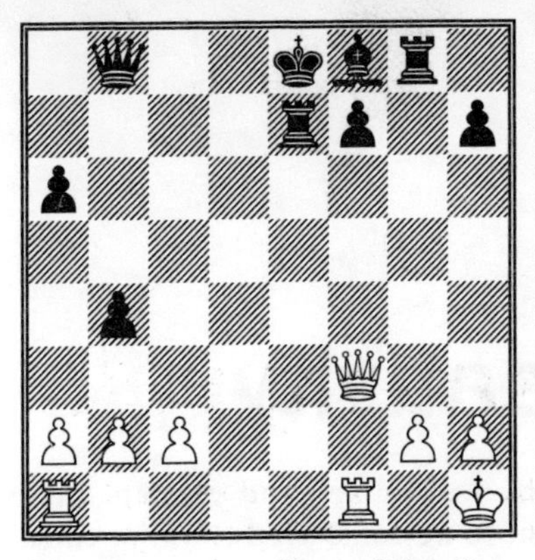

White to play in Fischer–Tal, Belgrade 1959. A classic example of a 'psychological trick'.

We mentioned, in the previous section, the Russian habit of writing down moves before playing them. This position is a classic example of that concept being turned inside out to the detriment of its practitioner. It is an even better example of a player winning a game through his Sumo face-off ability.

Fischer, as White, had sacrificed a piece. With Black's king in the centre and his pieces unco-ordinated, both players thought that the White attack should win, though neither had seen a clear path to victory. What happened next is beautifully explained by Tal himself in his autobiographical *The Life and Games of Mikhail Tal* (RHM Press, 1976): 'Fischer first wrote down the move 22.Rae1!, without doubt the strongest*, and wrote it not in his usual English notation [22.QR-K1] but in European, almost Russian! And not very deftly pushed the scoresheet towards me. "He's asking for an endorsement", I thought to myself, but how was I to react?'

Frowning, says Tal, was impossible. Smiling would look like an attempt at trickery, so he calmly got up and walked up and down the stage, even sharing a joke with Petrosian. Fischer meanwhile 'sat with a confused expression on his face'. Then he changed his mind and played 22.Qc6+? when after 22...Rd7 23.Rae1+ Be7 24.Rxf7 Kxf7 25.Qe6+ Kf8 26.Qxd7 Qd6 Black went on to win.

After that experience, Fischer always objected to the habit of writing moves down before playing them.

*In fact, Fischer later showed that Black can salvage a draw after 22.Rae1 Kd8! though he must play with supreme accuracy to do so.

creativity

In the good old days when men were men and gambits were mandatory if you did not want to be considered a wimp, chess was a creative pursuit. Brilliant players would conjure winning attacks out of thin air and nobody knew enough about the game to follow preconceived strategic plans. Eveything had to be worked out at the board.

Then came Steinitz and his theory of the accumulation of small advantages, and Dr Tarrasch and his pedantic rules for correct play, and opening theory and endgame theory, and computers and databases, until nowadays it seems that anyone can acquire the essentials of good chess by means of diligent study alone. Chess has moved from being an outlet for creative minds to a predominantly interpretative art. All the tactical ideas have been seen before, all the strategies are known; a player is left only with the task of assembling them to his liking.

Yet there is still room for creativity and we have seen one example in Section 45. While completely original concepts are rare, there is still enough opportunity in any game to combine the old ideas in a way that will set the opponent problems to solve. Kasparov found a way, in what looked like a sterile position, to create enough turmoil to push Karpov over the edge. The genius, on that memorable occasion, was to sense that the opportunity would arise in such a simple-looking position to create mayhem. The role of creativity was to find ways of piling different layers of tension on the position until it all became too much for Black to handle.

There was nothing original in any of the individual components of White's plan; his creative skill was to find a way of juggling them all in the air at the same time.

Chess is primarily an interpretative art, but there is still room in any game for real creativity to flourish.

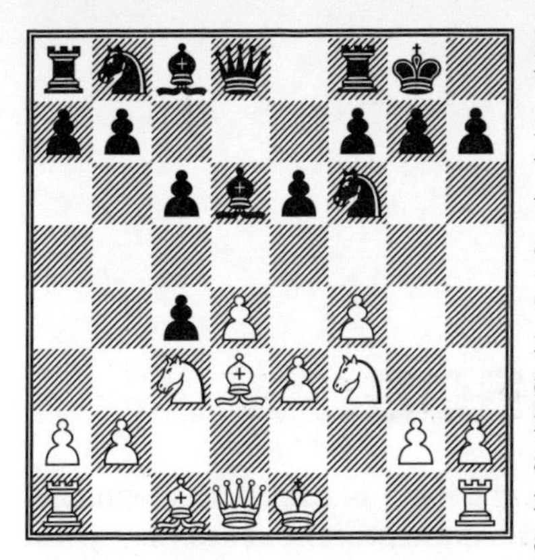

Black has just played dxc4. White, of course, will recapture with the bishop without thinking. After all, what else is there to think about?

Gyula Breyer, playing White in this position against Esser at Budapest 1917, did indeed find something else to think about. He played **1.Bb1!?** maintaining his control of e4 and planning a quick advance of the e-pawn. The game continued **1...b5** (1...c5! is a better challenge to White's idea) **2.e4 Be7 3.Ng5! h6 4.h4! g6 5.e5! hxg5 6.hxg5 Nd5.**

What does White have for his piece? There are clearly hopes of a successful attack down the h-file, but 7.Qg4 may be met by 7...Kg7 with the threat of Rh8. Now watch what happened: **7.Kf1!! Nxc3 8.bxc3 Bb7 9.Qg4 Kg7 10.Rh7+! Kxh7 11.Qh5+ Kg7 12.Qh6+ Kg8 13.Bxg6! fxg6 14.Qxg6+ Kh8 15.Qh6+ Kg8 16.g6 Rf7 17.gxf7+ Kxf7 18.Qh5+ Kg7 19.f5! exf5 20.Bh6+ resigns.** White wins after 20...Kh7 21.Bf4+ Kg7 22.Qh6+ Kg8 (or 22...Kf7 23.e6+) 23.Qg6+ Kh8 24.Ke2 Bh4 25.Rh1.

But what about that 7.Kf1 move? What was the point of it? Just look at the position after 16.g6. With the king still on e1, Black could have played 16...Bh4+ followed by Qe7. The idea therefore is completely logical – cut out the check to make the combination playable – but the notion that such a move might actually work is something totally original. This may be the only game in history in which a player has moved his king while still in the opening, to eliminate the possibility of a check in a variation nine moves later.

The Hungarian Gyula Breyer, incidentally, was one of the most imaginative chess minds of his time. He was one of the founders of the Hypermodern school of play, but died of heart disease when only 28.

chaos

The theory of chaos is one of the most beautiful developments in mathematics in recent years. At the heart of chaos theory lies the discovery that totally deterministic systems can still be essentially unpredictable. In other words, you can have a system that functions entirely according to known laws – so that if you know where everything is at any given moment, and how fast it is moving, and how much it weighs, and all its other relevant physical characteristics, then you can calculate where everything will be at any given time in the future – and it still turns out that you can, with the most accurate measuring equipment conceivable, still be wildly out in your calculations.

The reason is that it is possible for minute changes in the initial conditions to make vast changes in the end result. In the classic example, a butterfly flapping its wings in Tokyo can be the difference between fine weather and a hurricane in New York some time later. And even if you could take into account the effect of the wing flap, then one breath of the butterfly could throw out your calculations just as badly.

Chaos Theory seems sometimes to apply to chess too. You know where all the pieces are, yet still a hurricane whips up out of nowhere. There is, however, a real art in handling chaotic positions. The trick is to keep the complications going until there is a way to resolve them in your favour.

> **Don't worry if you can't see clearly through complications. Your opponent probably can't see through them either.**

One of the most common ways for strong players to defeat weaker ones is simply to create complications. The weaker player, feeling unsure of himself, resolves the complications and accepts a disadvantage. All the stronger player has to do is find a sympathetic butterfly ready to flap its wings and blow up a hurricane. The weaker player's lack of confidence will do the rest.

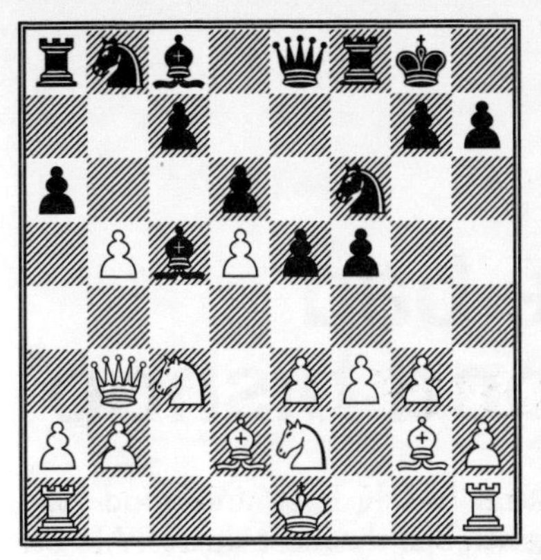

This position, from the 9th game of the Botvinnik–Bronstein match in 1951, was the start of one of the most chaotic episodes in world championship history. White has just captured a pawn on b5. Bronstein continued **1...Bd7**, having analysed the possible continuation 2.Na4 Ba7 3.b6! Bxa4 4.b7! Bxb3 and then discovering that 5...Bb6! 6.bxa8=Q Bxd5! leaves the newly promoted white queen trapped. Unfortunately, after 4...Bxb3 it is White's move not Black's, as Bronstein discovered after the moves **2.Na4 Ba7 3.b6 Bxa4 4.b7 Bxb3 5.bxa8=Q** had been played. 'My skin went all prickly,' he admitted, when he discovered that he needed two moves in a row, Bb6 and Bxd5, to trap the queen.

A rook down, Black's only hope now is chaos, so he continued **5...Bb6 6.axb3 Qb5 7.Nc3 Qxb3.** Now after 8.0-0, he has no real compensation for his rook, but Botvinnik wanted to do something to encourage his opponent to resign so played **8.Rxa6?! Nxa6 9.Qxa6.** White's queen is out and he is still a piece up. **9...Nxd5** (a piece for a pawn) **10.Qa4 Qxa4 11.Nxa4 Bxe3** (a piece for two pawns) **12.Bf1 Ra8! 13.b3** (13.Bc4 Rxa4 14.Bxd5+ Kf8 15.Bxe3 Ra1+ is the sort of thing to make White wish he had castled at move 8) **13...Bxd2+ 14.Kxd2 Kf8 15.Bd3 g6 16.Rc1 Rb8 17.Nc3 Nb4.** The hurricane has died down and Black, now ready to play c6, d5 and e4, not only saved the game quite comfortably, but almost won it.

Uncertainty is always the biggest enemy of the player with a winning position; the chaos approach is one good way of introducing that uncertainty.

the bad 'good bishop'

We have met good bishops and bad bishops and good 'bad bishops'. Here is the last of the set, and the most elusive. Almost all that we have said so far about bishops concerns their mobility and their influence on the empty squares of the board. A good bishop is one that is free to roam around or attack the enemy.

But bishops, like other pieces, may have defensive duties to perform as well as attacking ones. In general it may be the best policy to put your pawns on the opposite colour square from the bishop – if you do that, they will complement each other in their control of the board – but if your pawns are on black squares and the bishop on white ones, what is going to defend the pawns for you?

> A good bishop may be very poor indeed if it is unable to defend an important pawn when needed.

As usual, it's all a question of the correct balance between strategy and tactics. It's bad policy to put your pawns on the same colour square as your bishop just because you feel safer with all your pieces defending each other. But it's equally bad policy to put your pawns on the opposite colour square without checking carefully the tactics that may affect the safety of those pawns.

Of all the gradations of bishop, the bad 'good bishop' is the rarest of all, but it is wise to remember that such things can exist and to be alert for the possibility.

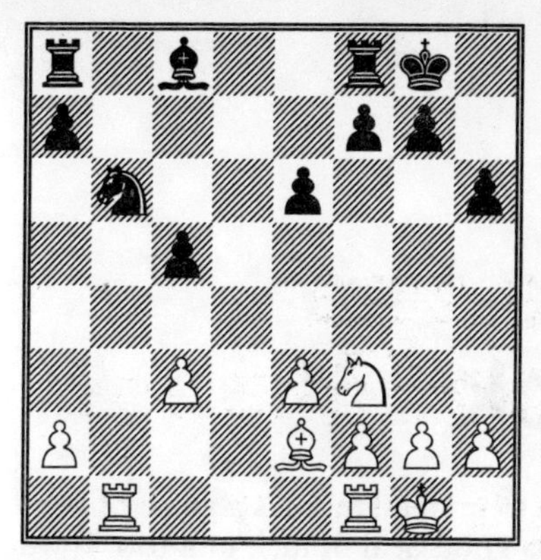

White to play in Karpov–Kasparov, 27th match game 1984. Does either side have anything at all to worry about in this almost symmetrical position?

Karpov sensed his prospects of attacking the pawn on c5 were better than Black's chances of attacking c3. Rather than invite exchanges of rooks down the d-file, he therefore played **1.Rfc1!** to bolster his pawn. There followed **1...Bb7** (natural, but the bishop would stand better on d7 to guard the b5 square) **2.Kf1 Bd5 3.Rb5! Nd7** (After 3...Bxa2 4.c4! Black finds his otherwise excellent bishop completely trapped.) **4.Ra5 Rfb8 5.c4! Bc6 6.Ne1! Rb4 7.Bd1!** The bishop is coming to b3 – where it looks very bad – in order to protect the a- and c-pawns and to block the b-file. The knight will then come to d3 and join the attack on c5. Note that 7.Nd3 would have been met by 7...Ra4, a move which is now prevented by the bishop.

The game continued **7...Rb7 8.f3 Rd8 9.Nd3 g5 10.Bb3!** (10.Nxc5 would be hurrying things: after 10...Nxc5 11.Rxc5 Rb2! 12.Rxc6 Rdd2 Black is doing well.) **10...Kf8 11.Nxc5 Nxc5 12.Rxc5** and White's extra pawn proved to be enough to win the game.

A little relaxation and a bishop that was too good for its own good were all it took for Black to lose this game.

98 luck

Is there luck in chess? We like to pretend that it's a game of pure skill, but we all know there's a good deal of luck in it too. If we really understood what was going on throughout a game, and genuinely felt that we deserved full credit for all the opponent's errors, then perhaps we could support the claim that skill is all that is involved. In practice, however, even the best players cannot control the game sufficiently not to be taken by surprise by unexpected occurrences.

When your steady pressure leads to the win of a pawn, and your opponent bales out into an endgame, it may be beyond the realms of calculation to know whether your extra pawn is enough to win. If the endgame turns out to be a draw with best play, you can justifiably consider that you were unlucky.

There is, however, one type of luck that is quite strongly within the control of the players. When a normally correct player commits a rare blunder, it is, of course, a piece of luck for his opponent, but there are ways of ensuring that you have more than your fair share of such lucky incidents.

> Some players rarely give their opponents a chance to blunder.

Technically correct players in particular tend to avoid the sort of trappy moves that lead to opponents blundering. Blunders rarely come unprovoked. If possible, one should, without compromising one's own position, leave a few things lying around that the opponent may trip over. You do not need to do anything so crude as setting traps. It is enough to believe that your opponent is capable of blundering to tip the scales of luck a little in your direction.

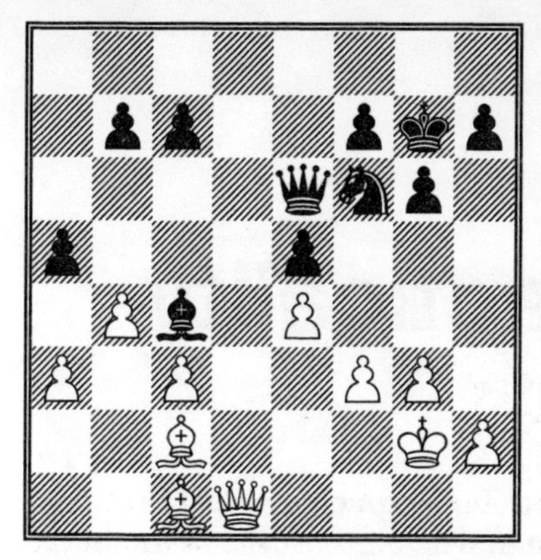

Confessions of a misspent youth, No. 3: from Andersson–Hartston, Hastings 1972–3. Black to play and create some luck.

Playing Black in this rather dull position, I wanted only to agree a draw and have a peaceful dinner without the worry of an adjourned game, but my opponent was renowned for his perseverance in level positions. My main cause for concern was the black squares on the K-side. While the idea of Qd2 and Qh6+ was not paticularly worrying – he has no means of following up the attack – I was more worried about his possible plan of Be3, Qd2 and Bh6+. I began considering the idea of advancing my pawns to h6 and g5 as a defensive reaction to his black-square attacking plan. But are the pawns more vulnerable on those squares? What if he later breaks up my formation by playing h4?

I simply did not know whether the pawns were better on h7 and g6 or h6 and g5, then I spotted a little trap contained in the latter formation. While not believing for a moment that my opponent would fall into it, I thought it might at least make him feel uneasy. So the game continued **1...h6 2.Be3 g5 3.Qd2 Ne8 4.Qd8 Nf6** (played with a shaking hand because I was genuinely nervous and short of time) **5.Qxc7??** (misinterpreting my tremulous gesture as a signal that I had blundered away the c-pawn) **5...Qh3+!**

My astonished opponent then looked at the board for a few seconds, looked up and said: 'It's mate.' After 6.Kxh3 Bf1 or 6.Kh1 Qf1+ 7.Bg1 Qxf3, he is quite right. A very lucky win for me – rarely, if ever, has Ulf Andersson been so generous to an opponent as he was when he took my c-pawn, but without my h6 and g5, he would not even have had the opportunity to be so kind.

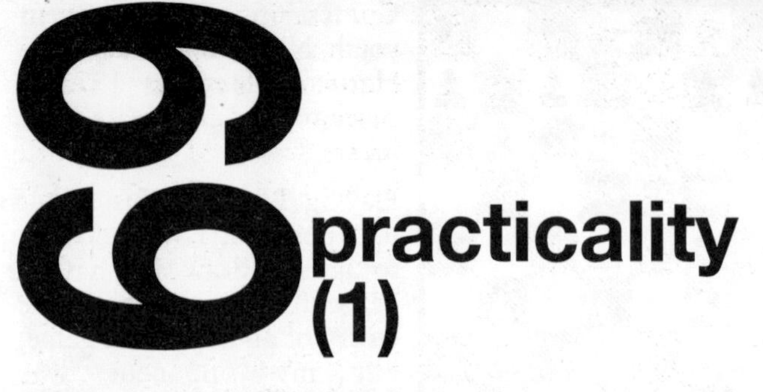

6 practicality (1)

We have mentioned before the Zen *koan* concerning the art of archery, which says that the man who aims for the centre of the target will win the prize, but the one who aims to win the prize will miss the target. At the very highest level of chess, a similar principle applies. Perfectionism is the only road to ultimate success. At anything below world championship level, however, practicality tends to fare better than perfectionism.

The practical player will not set himself unnecessary problems. He will not spend ages thinking about moves he is never going to play; he will not wallow in the joy of pondering the incalculable; he will not force himself to play with the utmost accuracy when the opponent has greater freedom of manoeuvre.

> Effective chess means quick decision-making and making life more difficult for the opponent than it is for yourself.

When you find yourself trying to choose between a pair of moves, or between two different strategies, it is easy to judge whether thinking is really going to help. There is a position after a dozen moves in the Ruy Lopez in which White has pawns on c3, d4 and e4 against Black on c5, d6 and e5. White must decide whether to block the centre by playing d5, open the d-file with dxe5, or maintain the tension by playing neither of those moves. After a hundred years of grandmaster practice, there is no consensus over which is best. Many decisions in individual games are much the same: to open the game or close it; to exchange or retreat; to move to this square or that one. You can tell at a glance whether thinking for a hundred years will bring you any closer to an answer. And if it won't you'll do best to rely on instinct.

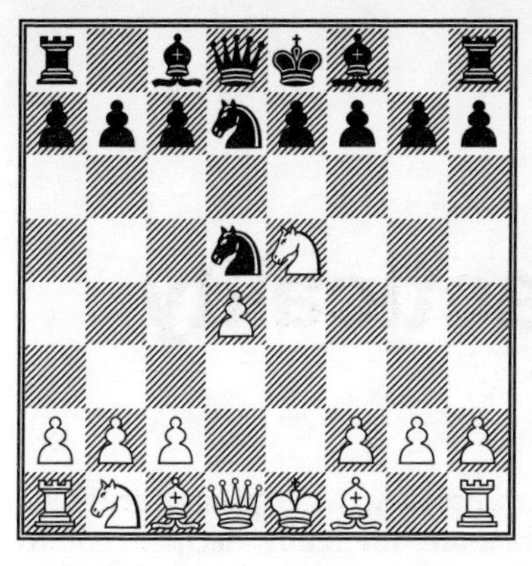

To sacrifice or not to sacrifice? A psychological blunder by a world champion. The position comes from Tal–Larsen, 5th match game 1965. Black has just played the cheeky 5...Nd7. As Tal says, 'If this had been in a simultaneous display, I would have decided that my opponent had simply overlooked the stroke 6.Nxf7 Kxf7 7.Qh5+, when, against his will, the black king is forced to go for a walk.' But this was a world championship semi-final, so Tal settled down to calculate everything, starting with 7...Ke6 8.c4 N5f6 9.d5+ Kd6 10.Qf7, then lurching off in another direction with 7...Ke6 8.g3!? b5 9.a4, but nothing led to any clear conclusions. An inherent belief in White's attack was contradicted by Tal's respect for his opponent and the knowledge that he must have analysed the whole thing very deeply. After 50 minutes, Tal had finally succeeded in convincing himself that Black might be able to defend the position, so he played 6.Bc4.

'Of course,' Tal wrote, 'the position did not require such consideration. Either my opponent's 'offer' should have been immediately declined, or else the problem should have been tackled without prejudice, and the knight sacrificed at f7.' For the rest of the game, Tal's thoughts kept returning to the variations he had analysed during those 50 wasted minutes. Playing listlessly, he adjourned in a distinctly inferior position and was extremely fortunate to save a draw the next day.

The decision not to sacrifice the knight had been quite justifiable, but thinking about it for 50 minutes was described by Tal as a 'psychological blunder'.

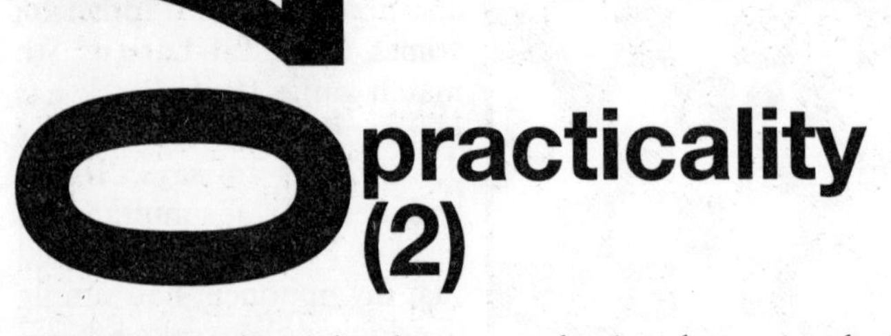

practicality (2)

Think again about that last example. At what point during his 50-minute thought do you imagine Tal really decided not to play Nxf7? The truth is that he had probably inwardly taken that decision within the first five minutes. But a good deal of chess thought works that way: for the most part you don't rationally and objectively work through the possibilities, compare the merits of individual moves, then take a decision about which is best. What you do is inwardly decide which move you want to play, then spend a good deal of time talking yourself into it. Like all the other important decisions in life – what job to take, where to live, which house to buy, whom to marry – your primary decision is based on gut instinct rather than objective analysis. But you back up your instinct by collecting as many bits of supportive evidence as you can find.

The problems (perhaps both in chess and life in general) arise when your instinct and your analysis reach different conclusions. You have reached a verdict, but the analytical evidence fails to substantiate it fully. In such circumstances, the wise old Argentinian grandmaster Miguel Najdorf had the answer:

> Play with your hands, not with your head.

When analysis and instinct are in conflict, you might as well trust instinct. (Unless, of course, the analysis does give clear cause for overruling your finer feelings.) For if you don't, you will not believe in the move you play and the resulting feeling of discomfort will lead to later errors anyway.

Playing a move that feels wrong is simply not the practical thing to do.

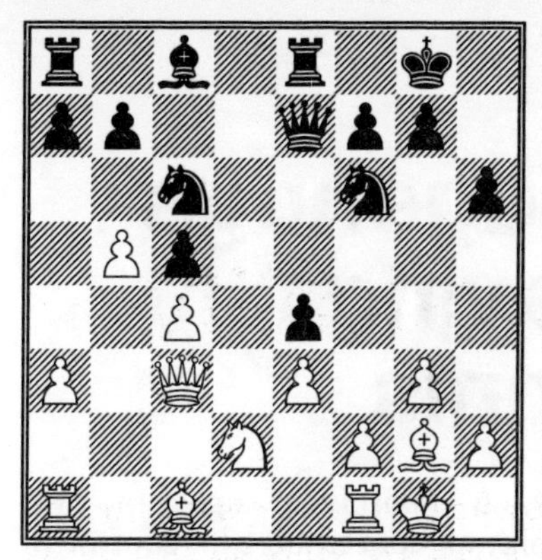

A severe case of practicality. Black to play in Kasparov–Anand, 4th match game 1995. His knight is attacked; where should he move it?

After 1...Nd8 or 1...Nb8, White continues with 2.Bb2 when the threat of 3.Nxe4 causes Black problems. The influence of White's queen and bishop on the long black diagonal is difficult to counter. Anand – by nature an intuitive player – took the practical decision to give up a pawn rather than let White have things all his own way. The game continued **1...Ne5(!) 2.Nxe4 Nf3+(!)**. There were two alternatives to this move: 2...Nxe4? 3.Bxe4 Nxc4 wins the pawn back but leaves Black with a miserable game after 4.Bd5, while 2...Bh3!? introduces huge complications. Anand explained that he looked first at Nf3+, considered it reasonable and decided to avoid wasting time by looking at anything else. There followed **3.Bxf3 Nxe4 4.Bxe4 Qxe4 5.f3 Qe7 6.e4 Be6 7.Be3** when Kasparov astonished everyone except his opponent by offering a draw – which was accepted. White is a pawn up, but quite unable to make progress. Black will play b6, f6 and Qf7 and White will be permanently tied to the defence of the c-pawn.

There were, however, at least two occasions on which White could have improved his play in this sequence. Instead of 4.Bxe4, he might have tried 4.Qc2 Bf5 (4...Qf6 5.Bxe4 Qxa1 6.Bb2 Qa2 7.Ra1 costs Black his queen) 5.Bb2 which looks precarious, but seems better for White since 5...Nxg3? fails to 6.Qc3! On White's final move of the game too, he should surely have tried 7.Bb2 f6 8.e5! countering Black's plans to attack c4 by launching his own aggressive action.

However, while analysis after the game cast doubt on Black's play, in the heat of battle White lost his way. Anand's practicality paid off handsomely, turning a difficult position into a comfortable draw in just a few moves.

hedgehogs playing tennis

In the 1960s and early 1970s, an important change came over the general attitude of top players concerning the control of space. Before then, it had been generally assumed that, all other things being equal, if White's pieces and pawns were spread over the first four ranks of the board, while Black's extended only over the back three, then White must have an advantage.

It gradually dawned on the collective grandmasterly mentality, however, that everything depends on the status of the empty rank between the two armies. A variety of what became known as 'hedgehog' formations began to appear in top-class play, with Black happily inviting his opponent to advance to the middle of the board, while identifying a clear demarcation zone on the rank in front. Black simultaneously prevented White from advancing further, while preparing to occupy that zone himself at a later stage and attack White's entire formation with the prickles of his hedgehog.

The cliché that several commentators fell into in describing the empty fifth rank in such formations was that it kept the sides apart 'just like the net in tennis'. It is, of course, nothing at all like the net in tennis. In tennis, you have to win a game before jumping over the net; in chess; it's the player who succeeds in jumping over the net first who will win the game.

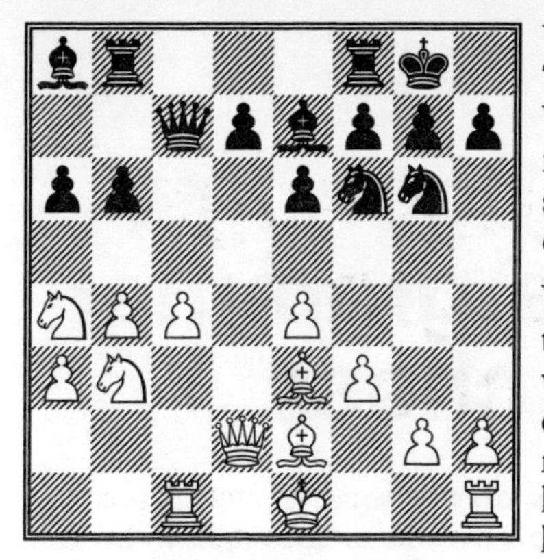

White to play in Honfi–Taimanov, Copenhagen 1965. What are both sides aiming for and how should White soften the prickles of his opponent's hedgehog?

White, with his four ranks to three advantage, needs to find a way to push forward into the demarcation zone; Black must resist any such advance, while looking for ways to challenge his opponent's extra space, perhaps with a later ...b5 or ...d5.

White would like to complete his development by castling, but 1.0-0 Bd6! causes some embarrassment in the defence of his h-pawn. Instead, he can push forwards immediately with 1.c5 b5 2.Nb6. Black then challenges the bold pawn with 2...d6, but 3.cxd6 Qxd6 4.Qxd6 Bxd6 5.Nxa8 Rxa8 is still in White's favour.

Instead, look what happened: **1.Qd4** (rushing to the net for a volley) **1...Nf4!** (drop shot) **2.Bxf4?** (retreating to the baseline with 2.Bf1 is better) **2...Qxf4 3.Nxb6 e5! 4.Qg1** (4.Qf2 is met by 4...Nxe4! 5.fxe4 Qxf2+ 6.Kxf2 Rxb6) **4...a5!** (bringing up chalk on the side-line) **5.g3 Qh6 6.c5 axb4 7.axb4 d5!** (taking control of the net) **8.Qf2 Rxb6! 9.cxb6 Bxb4+ 10.Kf1 dxe4** (jumping over the net) **11.Rc4 Bd6 12.Kg2 exf3+ 13.Bxf3 e4 14.Rxe4 Nxe4 15.Qd4 Nxg3! 16.Bxa8 Nxh1 White resigns.** Game, set and match. A triumph for the hedgehog and not like tennis at all.

2 the grammar of chess

With up to 32 pieces scattered over 64 squares, a chess position is not the sort of thing our rather feeble minds ought to be very good at coping with. A range of psychological experiments has shown that whatever concepts we are trying to juggle in our short-term memory, it's difficult to handle more than about seven of them. All the evidence suggests that we cope with chess by using similar skills to those utilized in language.

Just as letters group into words, and words into sentences and sentences into paragraphs, several chessmen may form a recognizable group (for example a knight on f3, bishop on g2, pawns on f2, g3, h3 and a king castled behind them all add up to a single 'word' in the chess language). As we play more and more chess, and – perhaps even more important – become familiar with more top-class games, our vocabulary grows. Not only that, but we begin to understand the relationships between the different words until the entire position makes some sort of sense.

We may even pursue the analogy to bring parts of speech to the chess language (I borrow this idea from the Japanese game of Shogi): the castled king and bishop in fianchetto, for example, may be seen as a noun. The idea of attacking it with ...Bg4 and Qd7 is, of course, rather an aggressive verb; while if White meets Bg4 with h3 and g4, chasing the bishop back to g6, then forces its exchange with Nh4, he is simply modifying the verb with an adverb.

> The strongest players are the ones who know most adverbs.

Acquiring the means to turn defence into attack, to modify your opponent's ambitions and to increase your armoury of strategic options is the highest level of chess grammar.

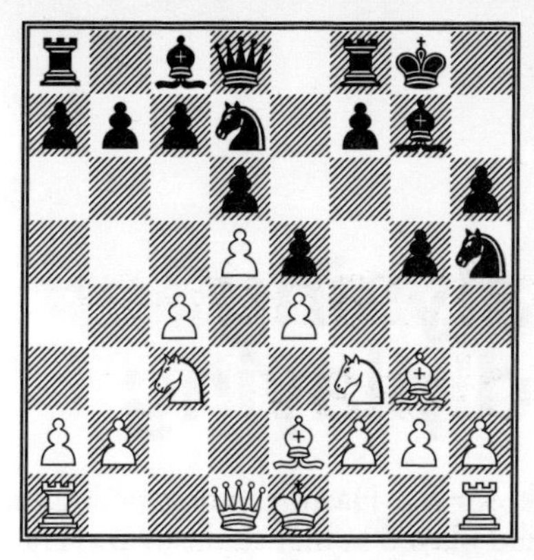

White to play in a common line of the King's Indian. Black has adopted a well-known noun on the K-side and hunted White's Bg5 verb with the h6, g5, Nh5 adverb. Where does the sentence go from here?

Before we get into the realms of gerunds and subjunctives, it is probably wise to drop the language metaphor, but there are still several inflections to the words now on the board that should form part of a player's vocabulary. One idea for White is 1.0-0 Nf4 (less rigid than Nxg3) 2.Nd2 planning white-square domination with Bg4. Another, as happened in the game Keres–Walther, Tel Aviv 1964, is **1.h4 g4** (or 1...Nf4?! 2.hxg5 hxg5 3.Qc2! Nxg2+ 4.Kd2 planning a huge attack down the g- and h-files) **2.Nh2 Nxg3 3.fxg3 h5 4.0-0 Bh6** when White's knight, lurking at h2, is always awaiting the opportunity of a piece sacrifice on g4. The game continued **5.Bd3 c6 6.Kh1 Nf6 7.Bc2 cxd5 8.cxd5 Ne8 9.Qe2 Ng7 10.Rf2 f5** (trying to break out before White's f-file pressure becomes annoying) **11.exf5 Nxf5 12.Bxf5 Bxf5 13.Raf1 Bg6 14.Nxg4!** (the knight's patience is at last rewarded) **14...hxg4 15.Qxg4 Kh7 16.h5 Bd3 17.Rxf8 Bxf8 18.Rf3 Bc2 19.Ne4 Kh8 20.Rf7 Qe8 21.Nxd6 Qa4 22.Qg5** and White's attack crashed home.

The whole idea of Bg5, h4, Nh2 and a piece sacrifice on g4 is now a standard plan against the King's Indian but, more importantly, the concept of using a bishop to provoke such a pawn advance, then attacking the pawns with h4, and even the eventual piece sacrifice is a meaningful paragraph that should be in the language of every strong player.

37 analysing and playing

When David Bronstein arrived for the Hastings tournament in 1975, it was the first time he had played in that traditional event for more than 20 years. In the first round, he met the former world junior champion Julio Kaplan and seemed to want to celebrate the occasion with a striking game. He achieved his wish with a fine win with the black pieces in 26 moves.

Ater the game, interest centred on a moment in the opening at which Bronstein had given his young opponent an opportunity to sacrifice a piece. One young English player (who subsequently became one of our top grandmasters) assailed Bronstein with several long and complex variations and a deluge of questions. 'How much did you analyse when you gave him the chance to sacrifice?' the young man asked. 'Did you analyse this line?' he said, shunting several pieces to and fro with great rapidity. 'Did you analyse the line he actually played?'

Bronstein treated the questions with a look of amused incomprehension. As the fourth or fifth 'Did you analyse...' question began, he held up a hand to stem the flood, then uttered a memorable rebuke:

> My dear boy, you don't analyse during a game. You analyze before a game and after a game. During a game you just play.

Which is more than just repeating what we have already said about trusting intuition over calculation. One acquires one's chess understanding by studying particular positions between games. You cannot learn to understand a particular type of position while engrossed in a life-and-death battle. You need the tranquility of a comfortable seat and your own favourite chess set to analyse effectively. When you get to the board for a competitive game, it is time to put your ideas and understanding to the test. That's playing, not analysing.

Playing beats thinking. This was the position in Kaplan–Bronstein, Hastings 1975–6, when things began to get interesting. White has just met ...c5 with d5. Black now played **1...f5** attacking the white knight and freeing the f6 square for knight or bishop. White, after a good deal of thought, played **2.dxe6** and after **2...fxe4** stopped to think again.

White must decide whether to sacrifice a piece with 3.exf7+ or keep material level with 3.exd7+. Kaplan talked himself out of the piece sacrifice, convincing himself that 3.exf7+ Kxf7 4.Qf4+ Nf6 5.Ne5+ Ke8 6.Bc4 Rf8 was good for Black. Bronstein later said that he did not trust this variation and would have invited a draw by perpetual check with 4...Kg7 5.Qg4+ Kf7.

The game continued **3.exd7+ Qxd7 4.Qc3 0-0 5.Nd2 Qf5 6.0-0-0 Qxf2.** Now, says Bronstein, 7.Bc4 must be correct. Instead, he again made the mistake of re-establishing material equality: **7.Nxe4? Qf4+ 8.Nd2 Bg4 9.Bd3 Rae8 10.Re1 Bg5 11.Ref1 Qe3 12.h3 Be2 13.Rf5 Bh6 14.Bxe2 Qxc3 15.bxc3 Rxe2 16.Rd5 Rxd2 17.Rxd2 Rd8 18.Rhd1 c4! White resigned.** When he runs out of pawn moves, he must lose a piece.

Both at move 3 and at move 7 in this sequence, White played moves that were against his natural inclinations because he could not produce hard evidence that his intended sacrifices were correct. Too much analysis, not enough playing.

24 the meta-rules of strategy

Every generation of chess players learns a little more about the game than the one that preceded it. The most eloquent of them try to explain their ideas in new manuals on the game. Yet each new exposition seems to lag one generation behind in its explanations. Howard Staunton, the great English champion of the mid-19th century, wrote fine books of detailed analysis of such romantic openings as the King's Gambit and Evans Gambit, yet in his own games he pioneered the sort of cautious positional chess that only became fashionable some 70 years later.

Emanuel Lasker, the second official world champion, explained and extolled the scientific principles that his predecessor, Wilhelm Steinitz, had discovered in his own games, yet Lasker played with all the insight of a recklessly brilliant gambler. He was the first to understand the true nature of the chess struggle and the tensions it creates in the human psyche, yet his writings are models of objectivity and lucidity. Mikhail Botvinnik's annotations imbue his games with authority and inevitability, yet he understood better than anyone the nature of the personal conflict between the two players involved in any game.

The fluidity of chess knowledge ensures that this must always be so. We seem able to crystallize our thoughts into stated principles only when our understanding has moved beyond them towards the underlying meta-principles. In other words:

> You can't play good chess just by applying rules and principles.

All the advice and explanations given in this or any other chess book will not, in itself, make you play better. I hope, however, that it will help to guide you towards a better understanding of the game.

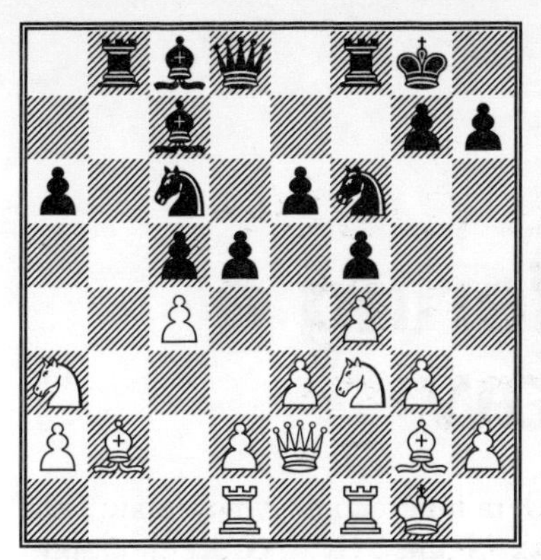

White's two fianchettoed bishops, his restrained centre pawns and his eccentrically developed knight on a3 bear all the hallmarks of the hypermodern school of the 1920s, yet this position comes from the game Staunton–Williams, London 1851.

It's White to play, and remember we are in an era of dashing attacks and brilliancy prizes. How do you imagine the game continued? Just watch.

1.Bxf6! Qxf6 2.cxd5 exd5 3.d4! Envisaging this pawn move, White first exchanged his black-squared bishop to ensure that it would not become bad (though it was another 50 years before anyone came up with the concept of a 'bad bishop'). He also gives himself a backward pawn (another concept not yet invented) on e3 which can be shielded (perhaps an idea first enunciated by Nimzowitsch in the 1920s) by a knight moving to e5.

There followed **3...c4 4.Ne5 Nb4** and now Staunton played a neat little combination: **5.Naxc4! dxc4 6.a3** when Black must lose back his knight since 6...Nd3 7.Nxc4 leaves it trapped. The game continued **6...Bxe5 7.dxe5 Qf7 8.axb4 Rxb4 9.Rd6** with a strategically winning position to White thanks to his command of the d-file and passed e-pawn. The remaining moves were 9...Bb7 10.e6 Qc7 11.Rd7 Qc8 12.Qd1 Bc6 (12...Bxg2 would have been met by 13.Qd4!) 13.Bxc6 Qxc6 14.Qd4 Rf6 15.Rd6 Qb5 16.Rd8+ Rf8 17.Rxf8+ Kxf8 18.Qd6+ Ke8 19.Rd1 resigns.

offering a draw

In football, they play for 90 minutes come what may, then sometimes settle matters with extra time and a penalty shoot-out. In cricket, they play for five days then call it a draw because it is raining. Only in chess can the two combatants agree to call off hostilities by mutual agreement whenever they think it appropriate.

A draw offer may be a simple acceptance of an inevitable result of a dead level position. It may be a sign of cowardice in the face of unpredictable dangers. It may even be a sign that there is an important football match on television in half an hour.

A strategic draw offer may come from a player whose advantage has begun to slip. Under such circumstances, it may serve as a way to determine the opponent's intentions and incite oneself to fight for the half-point.

As this book draws to a close, however, it seems the right thing to end with a peaceful outcome and a final homily. In his superb book on the 1953 Candidates' Tournament, David Bronstein tells the story of a draw offer in the game between Isaac Boleslavsky and Miguel Najdorf. After Boleslavsky had played an uncharacteristically insipid line as White against the King's Indian Defence, Najdorf enquired:

'Are you playing for a draw?'
'No,' replied Boleslavsky.
'So you're playing for a win?'
'Mm, not really.'
'Don't tell me you're playing for a loss?'
'I am just making the moves,' explained Boleslavsky, 'that the position demands.'

Which is exactly what we should all try to do, whatever the position.

Just make the moves that the position demands.

The Boleslavsky–Najdorf game, incidentally, ended in a draw.

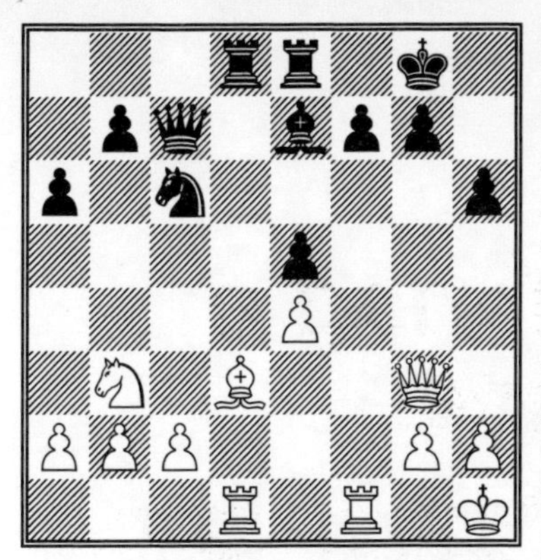

This position, from Hartston–Penrose, London 1963, is the last and most damning of my confessions from a misspent youth. My opponent had looked nervous when making his rook to d8 to reach this position, so I thought it a good moment to offer a draw. He immediately accepted. Why?

The answer is because White has a forced win. After 1.Rxf7! Kxf7 2.Bc4+ Kf8 3.Rf1+ Bf6 4.Rxf6+! gxf6 5.Qg8+ Ke7 6.Qe6+ Kf8 7.Qxf6+ Black is mated next move.

The chess writer Harry Golombek was once approached by a contestant in the British Ladies Championship. 'Mr Golombek,' the lady said, 'I should very much value your opinion on a matter relating to a game I just finished.'

He encouraged her to proceed.

'Well, we reached a position in which my opponent had a forced mate in three and she offered me a draw. I reasoned that if she was offering a draw, she could not have seen the mate; and if she didn't find the mate, then I would stand a good chance of winning the game. So I declined the offer and went on to win. Tell me, Mr Golombek, was this good chess?'

I don't know what answer the lady received, but it seems as good a problem as any with which to leave the reader.

your next move

So now you have read and understood all the lessons in this book, giving you 75 more (or at least improved) weapons in your chess armoury. Will this make you a better player? You may well feel cheated if it doesn't. The book, after all, is called *Teach Yourself Better Chess*. But hang on just one moment: look at that title again. It is not *Teach Yourself To Play Better Chess*. What I have tried to do, is introduce the ideas that will enable you to understand chess better – to get a grasp of what good chess is all about. Now you must learn how to use those weapons and that can come only from experience.

If there is one thing I have tried to stress throughout this book it is that good chess is not simply a matter of applying strategic principles and rules. The rules underlying good chess are, as you have probably now grasped, often mutually contradictory or individually paradoxical. The real art lies in sensing which rules apply to which positions.

So how should you set about improving your practical chess skills? There are three main directions to follow:

Study

There are thousands of books on chess – from books on individual openings to books of specific endgames; games collections of the great masters; collections of games from world championship matches or important tournaments; books on winning combinations, and even a book called *How to Lose at Chess*. Playing through entire games or the crucial parts of games will help develop your fluency in much the same way as reading a book in a foreign language can help hone your linguistic skills.

We all have our own taste in writing styles, which makes me reluctant to recommend specific books. I have always preferred well-written books, such as Richard Reti's classic *Masters of the Chessboard*, or Aaron Nimzowitch's *My System*, which offer long and detailed explanations of the thoughts behind each move. Other people, I know, prefer symbols and long strings of chess moves to wordy explanations. Just find a style that does not intimidate you and read as much as you have time for.

I have deliberately steered clear of almost all discussion of individual opening variations in this book. In practice, however, selecting a suitable opening repertoire is a high priority. Again this will come most easily by playing through games of the great masters. Occasionally, you will find a game that you feel in tune with from start to finish – and that is as good a guide as any that the opening is one that might suit you. So play it, try it for size, and then think about looking it up in an openings manual.

A subscription to a chess magazine is another way to achieve regular doses of chess wisdom and information. The leading British publications are *The British Chess Magazine* (www.bcmchess.co.uk) and *Chess* (www.chess.co.uk) whose magazines and websites also offer detailed information of current chess news and activities.

In the US, the same service is provided by a variety of magazines including the official publication of the US Chess Federation, *Chess Life*. (www.uschess.org/about/clife.html).

Play

Understanding the principles of good chess is one thing; applying them is another. No amount of study can prepare you for taking decisions in the heat of battle. The game of chess is a conflict. At an obvious level it is a conflict between the two players; at another level, as I have tried to show throughout this book, it is a conflict between a host of complex elements that make up a position. Precise calculation and fuzzy judgment will only rarely leave you in no doubt what is the best move. The stress of making decisions under such uncertainty is what makes chess such an exciting and infuriating competitive game.

So where can you find an opponent? A friend or group of friends who share your interest is an asset in the early stages of learning, but it is very easy for all of you to get stuck at the same level. You should be constantly striving to find opponents better than yourself (but not too much better) to test your ideas and provide the impetus for you to improve. Joining a chess club is one way. Your national chess federation will be able to point you in the direction of your local one, as well as providing details of any tournaments in your area. For British and American readers, the following details may be helpful:

The British Chess Federation
The Watch Oak
Chain Lane
Battle
East Sussex
TN33 0YD
Tel: 01424 775222
www.bcf.org.uk

The US Chess Federation
USCF 3054 NYS Route 9W
New Windsor
NY 12553
Tel: 1-845-562-8350
www.uschess.org

The Internet

As the above addresses may suggest, the game of chess is flourishing on the Internet, with a wide variety of opportunities to find an opponent for an online game, or follow important international games live, or download archives of historical games. Here are some good places to start:

www.chess.co.uk is the site of *Chess* magazine, as mentioned above, as well as the host of The Week In Chess (www.chess.co.uk/twic/twic.html), the most comprehensive and up-to-date source of international chess news. The links from this page also provide an excellent starting point for anyone wanting to set off into the jungle of Internet chess.

www.chesscafe.com is an excellent online chess magazine with a range of articles to suit all tastes and ability levels. From grandmaster annotations to a Question and Answer section for struggling amateurs, this is an excellent resource for anyone wanting to widen their chess horizons.

www.chessclub.com is the Internet Chess Club, an ever-growing community of chess players around the world. Unlike the two sites mentioned above, this is a subscription service with a membership around the same level as the average chess club – but it does offer a week's free trial with no obligation. After logging on you may join in their constant stream of tournaments, eavesdrop on other players' games, or seek a friendly game from one of the many thousands of players logged on at any moment of the night or day. Usually you will pick up an opponent within seconds. After a few games, you will find you have established a rating, which will enable you to be paired with opponents of suitable strength.

Whatever you do, keep playing and keep studying, and your Better Chess will become better still.

index